P9-CLD-043

CROSSCURRENTS *Modern Critiques*

CROSSCURRENTS *Modern Critiques*
Harry T. Moore, *General Editor*

Irving Malin

New American Gothic

WITH A PREFACE BY

Harry T. Moore

Carbondale

SOUTHERN ILLINOIS UNIVERSITY PRESS

16779

Illinois Central College
Learning Resouce Center

Copyright © 1962 by Southern Illinois University Press.
All rights reserved.
Library of Congress Catalog Card Number 62–15005
Printed in the United States of America
Designed by Andor Braun

FIRST PUBLISHED, OCTOBER 1962
SECOND PRINTING, MARCH 1964

for my father and grandmother
who cannot read this

BUSILY EXTROVERTED America has produced its quota of "Gothic" writers, the explorers of their own private worlds, who range from Charles Brockden Brown through Poe and up to the "newer" group which Irving Malin deals with in the present book: Truman Capote, James Purdy, Flannery O'Connor, John Hawkes, Carson McCullers, and J. D. Salinger. Mr. Malin doesn't emphasize causality; he makes no attempt to discover why these authors are what they are, but rather he takes them as they are and explores their tortuous inwardness in order to chart (his word) their characteristics and tendencies.

He does so, I think, to the profit of us all. He investigates the Gothic from a somewhat different angle than that of William Van O'Connor in his book in the Crosscurrents series, The Grotesque: An American Genre, and for the most part Mr. Malin deals with different authors than those Mr. O'Connor writes of. Mr. Malin is concerned with a specific small group, and when he finishes his charting of their work, he then provides an evaluation of it, about which more later.

In regard to Mr. Malin's lack of interest in the causal and in the sociological, it might be pointed out that while literature can often help us to understand certain features of a time and place, its truest function is just to be literature; it most importantly exists for its own sake. Mr. Malin is a critic who doesn't use literature instrumentally, but rather leaves its socio-historical applications to others and goes on to provide us with a study of writers as writers. Yet he drops many illuminating hints by the way, and his book has the general effect of making us understand American life more fully than we did before. But, once again, this is only an incidental aspect of his work.

As Mr. Malin points out, the newer Gothic writers are closely related to Poe, but far removed from Howells; yet they are in the mainstream of American literature (and surely Howells is, too, in another part and perhaps at a different depth). To them, "the psyche is more important than society," and usually they write about a microcosm: a Southern town, a city house, an army camp in peacetime, or Central Park. Such writers are of course at the opposite end of modern literature from, say, Dos Passos, who in his early work showed occasional tendencies toward the Gothic, but who carefully relegated all inwardness and subjectivity to "Camera-Eye" fragments scattered across the enormous sociological surface of his U.S.A. trilogy.

The true Gothic on the other hand is essentially and continuously subjective, presenting reality as a distorting mirror. In the past, as Mr. Malin points out, the older American Gothic projected its narcissism powerfully, "but new American Gothic uses heroes who cannot even proclaim their narcissism in strong ways." As Mr. Malin shows in his chapter on "Self-Love," the narcissism of these characters drives them so deeply into their private worlds that they become totally isolated. Mr. Malin—again it is helpful to use his word—charts this isolation in the works of the authors he is considering, three of whom—McCullers, Capote, and Flannery O'Connor—belong to the Southern group which has produced so many "dark" writers in our time. He deals with his three Southern authors in this "Self-Love" section, but there he also gets into the work of the other trio—Salinger, Purdy, and Hawkes—in each case demonstrating how the self-love of the people they write about leads to a mechanization of character. And in doing so he points out an irony: these authors manifest a creativity which their heroes lack.

Mr. Malin also deals with the family as treated by the newer Gothic writers, whose characters invariably use their narcissism in their attempts to destroy that unit of human organization. Here again Mr. Malin provides a close reading of his six representative Gothic authors, and once more he gives us some valuable insights after juxtaposing their works. In his chapter "Three Images," he explores the recurring symbols of the Gothic which have been handed down from Horace Walpole, "Monk" Lewis, and Mrs. Radcliffe: "the haunted castle, the voyage into the forest, and the reflection." To these earlier authors—and Mr. Malin adds Hawthorne and the Gothic writings of Henry James—such symbols were objective correlatives of the psyche; Mr. Malin shows how the later Gothic writers use the same images in their more private world of narcissism and antagonism to the family. Here he draws upon points established in earlier parts of the book, working them into the larger thematic development that brings him to the climax of his study.

And yet there are a few more things for Mr. Malin to say, as he indicates in his "Conclusion." However valuable the study of trends and characteristics may be, the qualitative question always underlies such explorations: How well do the authors being analyzed handle their material?

Throughout, Mr. Malin gives incidental evaluations,

but he reserves his last chapter for a full consideration of what is after all the heart of criticism, literary merit. This is more than a matter of merely analyzing theme and subject.

In that final chapter, Mr. Malin examines the excellences and defects of the six writers dealt with in the book. At this point there would be no purpose in spoiling the reader's pleasure by offering a summary of Mr. Malin's findings, though his treatment of one of these authors might be mentioned: Salinger. Mr. Malin doesn't overrate Salinger, which is refreshing and good; perhaps regrettably, he doesn't sufficiently expand the catalogue of Salinger's shortcomings, one of the most notable of which he merely mentions: monotone. Earlier in the book, Mr. Malin had shown what is important in Salinger by looking at his themes, which have a typicality, at least for temporary and permanent adolescents—those who are probably the most susceptible, in our society, to the newer Gothic. Salinger's books have raged through the best-seller lists, and they have drawn the admiration of various critics, who sometimes behave as if Salinger were another Stendhal or Proust. Actually, he is merely another slick writer who, like Wouk in his different way, has become a vogue.

Since everyone is looking for Salinger anecdotes, here's one connected with the present book. Readers who find in its text some occasional and useful quotations from the other five authors discussed may observe that Salinger's own words never appear here. Usually a critic in a serious work may employ a certain amount of quotation—this is known as fair usage—or the publishers of the authors under consideration may grant him the courtesy of incorporating pertinent passages as he needs to do so; but, when approached in relation to the matter, Salinger's publishers said that he didn't permit quotation of his work. How could this handicap be overcome? Only by obtaining direct permission from J. D. Salinger, who of course doesn't answer communications addressed to him. Now, since he does, however condescendingly, allow himself to be published, why does he want to handicap other writers who are commenting upon what he has publicly written? One answer may be that Salinger inhabits a world as unreal as his fiction seems (to a minority of us) to be; another answer may be that Salinger has ascended to the plane of the fat lady whom, in Franny and Zooey, he so ludicrously designates as Christ. The splendid isolation of the artist is perhaps too seldom attained in noisy America, but it seems to some of us, at least, that the man who publishes has certain elementary obligations of courtesy. To be a shy Emily Dickinson or Franz Kafka is quite another matter; they published very little while alive, holding back their deserved reputations for a posthumous blooming, amid a posterity that couldn't bother them. In short, they didn't try to have it both ways at once. But perhaps Emily Dickinson and Kafka don't belong in this little argument at all, since they are writers who apparently will last.

Some of Mr. Malin's other authors may also last, particularly Carson McCullers and Flannery O'Connor. John Hawkes and James Purdy, despite minority recognition, haven't come into their own yet, and it's too early to attempt a judgment. Truman Capote has talent, but he too often skids along surfaces; perhaps he will some day return to the true Gothic vein of Other Voices, Other Rooms.

Anyhow, these half dozen men and women discussed in the present volume represent some interesting, often fascinating, developments in recent American literature; and Irving Malin deserves our appreciation for the way in which he has charted these developments.

We are at a point in American literary study at which the validity of examining one's contemporaries has been challenged; a new school is arising which looks upon the contemporary merely as the temporary, a school which wants a disciplined return to the Classics. Perhaps we have overdone the moderns, but it must be said that, since imaginative literature is an index to the consciousness of an age, we can come closer to an understanding of that consciousness with the help of books such as the present, whose primary function, however, is to discover literary values; and certainly Mr. Malin has achieved that.

May 30, 1962   HARRY T. MOORE

ACKNOWLEDGMENTS

IN ADDITION to the sources given in the notes, special acknowledgment is made to the following publishers for permission to quote from the works indicated.

Doubleday & Company, Inc.: *The American Novel and Its Tradition* by Richard Chase, copyright 1957 by Richard Chase.

Farrar, Straus & Cudahy, Inc.: *The Violent Bear It Away* by Flannery O'Connor and *Malcolm* by James Purdy.

Harcourt, Brace and World, Inc.: *Wise Blood* and *A Good Man Is Hard to Find* by Flannery O'Connor.

Harper's Bazaar: "The Enduring Chill" by Flannery O'Connor.

Houghton Mifflin Company: *The Ballad of the Sad Café, The Member of the Wedding, Reflections in a Golden Eye,* and *The Heart Is a Lonely Hunter* by Carson McCullers.

J. B. Lippincott Company: *Color of Darkness* by James Purdy.

The Macmillan Company: "The Fiction Writer and His Country" by Flannery O'Connor in *The Living Novel* (1957), edited by Granville Hicks.

McGraw-Hill Book Company, Inc.: *After the Lost Generation: A Critical Study of the Writers of Two Wars* by John W. Aldridge. Copyright 1951 by the McGraw-Hill Book Company.

New Directions, Publishers: *Charivari* from *New Directions* 11 and *The Cannibal* by John Hawkes, copyright 1949 by New Directions; *The Beetle Leg*, copyright 1951 by John Hawkes; *The Goose on the Grave*, copyright 1954 by John Hawkes; *The Lime Twig*, copyright 1961 by John Hawkes; Introduction to *The Lime Twig*, copyright 1961 by New Directions; *Color of Darkness*, copyright 1957 by James Purdy.

Random House, Inc.: *Other Voices, Other Rooms* and *A Tree of Night and Other Stories* by Truman Capote.

CONTENTS

New American Gothic

1 INTRODUCTION

JOHN W. ALDRIDGE has effectively stated the case against new American Gothic. In his essay on Capote and Buechner, appropriately subtitled "The Escape into Otherness," he writes:

> They have also escaped the problem of giving significance to evil and guilt within the context of a valueless society. They have been able to create a separate and private moral context for each of their books and to find a meaning for the moral dilemma of their characters within that context. It should not matter if the meaning they find lacks reference in the social world. By making their books something other than reflections of that world, they should, by rights, have relieved themselves of all obligations to it. But in even the most perfect novel of privacy there always comes a time when purely contextual meaning ceases to be enough and one begins to wish for a kind of significance that will expand beyond itself and illuminate the universal issues of life.[1]

Mr. Aldridge is correct: Capote and the others do not deal with political tensions; they explore a world in which characters are distracted by private visions. But a problem immediately arises: Are these visions so unusual? I think a valid argument can be made for the fact that we look inward as much as we do at Laos. The writer who illuminates the terror of the "buried life" performs a necessary and even vital service. Mr. Aldridge wants an examination of the "universal issues of life," but he does not define them. Perhaps my disagreement with him lies in the fact that "privacy" and "universal" are vague words. Surely the buried life is always tied to some sort of social conditioning: it conditions and is conditioned by "others." The writers of new American Gothic are aware of tensions between ego and super-ego, self and society; they study the *field* of psychological conflict.

Apparently Mr. Aldridge wants fiction to be "social." He wants "true" descriptions of Chicago; he wants economic strife or social guilt at the center. This kind of realism can constrict the imagination and its illumination of the buried life. Often, inferior writers who are tempted by such realism do not look under the materialistic surface—which does not prevent them from expounding their philosophies. This is the case with Dreiser at his worst, and Lionel Trilling's stricture against him can apply equally well to other realists: "When he thinks like, as we say, a philosopher, he is likely to be not only foolish but vulgar. He thinks as the modern crowd thinks when it decided to think." [2] Of course, such novels as *The Adventures of Augie March* offer social truths without sacrificing imagination and intellect. But much can be said for the "timeless" quality of *Malcolm:* "In front of one of the most palatial hotels in the world, a very young man was accustomed to sit on a bench which, when the light fell in a certain way, shone like gold." This "pure" scene can be anywhere; is it private or universal?

New American Gothic is in the mainstream of American fiction. Richard Chase has argued persuasively that the characteristic works of the American imagination have been romances rather than the novels Mr. Aldridge seems to admire:

The American novel tends to rest in contradictions and among extreme ranges of experience. When it attempts to resolve contradictions, it does so in oblique, morally equivocal ways. As a general rule it does so either in melodramatic actions or in pastoral idyls, although intermixed with both one may find the stirring instabilities of "American humor." . . . By contrast the English novel has followed a middle way. It is notable for its great practical sanity, its powerful, engrossing composition of wide ranges of experience into moral centrality and equability of judgment. Oddity, distortion of personality, dislocations of normal life, recklessness of behavior, malignancy of motive—these the English novel has included. Yet the profound poetry of disorder we find in the American novel is missing, with rare exceptions, from the English.[3]

Regard this phrase: the "poetry of disorder." New American Gothic is close to Poe and far removed from Howells. It believes that the psyche is more important than society or, if this is a bit extreme, that the disorder of the buried life must be charted. And this disorder does not require a large area of society in which to reveal itself. Gothic employs a microcosm: an army camp in peacetime, Skulley's Landing, a crazy house on 63rd Street, and Central Park. But in the microcosm there is enough room for irrational (and universal) forces to explode.

What are these forces? New American Gothic is primarily concerned with love, knowing "that there can be no terror without the hope for love and love's defeat." [4] The typical hero is a weakling. The only way he can escape from that anxiety which constantly plagues him is through compulsion. He "loves" others because he loves himself: he compels them to mirror his desires. Love for him is an attempt to create order out of chaos, strength out of weakness; however, it simply creates monsters. Although it is easy to dismiss the cripples and homosexuals in new American Gothic as sensational cardboard figures, they are frequently powerful symbols of disfiguring, narcissistic love. They "work" as does Frankenstein.

The concern with narcissism accounts in great part for the quality of Gothic. Gothic is flat, stylized, and almost inhuman because it severely limits personality. Characters cannot be "well-rounded" while they are obsessed with themselves. Ihab Hassan explains the matter this way: "The Gothic insists on spiritualization, the spiritualization of matter itself, and it insists on subjectivism." [5] It seeks, in other words, to demonstrate how weaklings read meanings into matter, meanings that reflect their own preoccupations. *Reality becomes a distorted mirror.* Sherwood Anderson describes the process in *Winesburg, Ohio:*

> Hundreds and hundreds were the truths and they were all beautiful.
>
> And then the people came along. Each as he appeared snatched up one of the truths and some who were quite strong snatched up a dozen of them.
>
> It was the truths that made the people grotesques. The old man had quite an elaborate theory concerning the matter. It was his notion that the moment one of the people took one of the truths to himself, called it his truth, and tried to live his life by it, he became a grotesque and the truth he embraced became a falsehood.

New American Gothic uses grotesques who love themselves so much that they cannot enter the social world except to dominate their neighbors.

Gothic narcissism extends far back into American fiction and accounts for some of the qualities Mr. Chase mentions. In *The Blithedale Romance,* for example, we are told that Hollingsworth has a philanthropic dream to construct an edifice for criminals. We are not really informed why this particular dream is formed or why it should become compulsive. Hawthorne's description centers on Hollingsworth's *growing* monomania, which Coverdale discovers to be caused by immense, monstrous self-love. *Once we grant its existence,* the narcissism is powerfully rendered:

> He was not altogether human. There was something else in Hollingsworth besides flesh and blood . . .
>
> This is always true of those men who have surrendered themselves to an overwhelming purpose. It does not so much impel them from without, nor even operate as a motive power within, but grows incorporate with all they think and feel. . . . They will keep no friend, unless he make himself the mirror of their purpose. . . . They have an idol to which they consecrate themselves high-priest, and deem it holy work to offer sacrifices of whatever is most precious, and never once seem to suspect . . . that this false deity, in whose iron features, immitigable to all the rest of mankind, they see only benignity and love, is but a spectrum of the very priest himself, projected upon the surrounding darkness.

Ahab is another ancestor. His compulsive design regards Moby Dick as the "wall," the "mask," through which he must strike, so that he can relieve himself of inferiority. Ahab views the environment narcissistically as a mirror of his own need, and dream, to impose his will without discrimination. He does not see Moby Dick as a living creature, both good and evil, only as an "instrument" to be manipulated.

Note the crucial difference. The ancestors are "great" in their narcissism; Ahab especially becomes Faustian. But new American Gothic uses heroes who cannot even proclaim their narcissism in strong ways. Only Hazel Motes of *Wise Blood* has the energy of self-love and self-hatred in the epic proportions of the old lovers.

The family is crucial in new American Gothic. There are several reasons for this: disfiguring love is often learned at home. Parents see themselves in their children but forget about self-expression on the part of the young; they want to mold unformed personalities. Children, on the other hand, become narcissistic because of their need to find and love themselves in a cold environment. New American Gothic employs the family as a microcosm: the family dramatizes the conflict between private and social worlds, ego and super-ego. Almost every work in the canon contains family terror. It is evident in *The Heart Is a Lonely Hunter* and *Other Voices, Other Rooms,* "Uncle Wiggily in Connecticut," "Color of Darkness," *The Beetle Leg,* and *The Violent Bear It Away.*

Although the writers of new American Gothic employ Freudian principles (consciously or unconsciously) in their use of the family, they are probably influenced by the old Gothic of "Monk" Lewis and the American followers of the tradition: Poe, Hawthorne, Melville, and Henry James. In *Pierre,* for example, we find the Gothic family. Relationships are distorted. Pierre addresses his domineering mother as sister; he looks at his dead father as "good." In both relationships Pierre is made to be more aware of himself than of his parents as such. He is narcissistic; he sees himself in his mother and father. And he desires a sister, not a brother, because his personal vision is effeminate —he wants to see himself in the sister. Mrs. Glendinning has helped to make Pierre an image of herself; she has molded him from birth to reflect her ideals. She distrusts Pierre's love for young women as a shattering of the narcissistic mirror.

"The Pupil" also shows conflict in the family. The parents in the story are authoritarian—they try to impose their disordered, bourgeois patterns upon their children. They simply look at their child, Morgan, as a quaint "genius." Although Morgan is the intellectual master of the situation, he lacks emotional control or any power to fight the situation, except through irony. He is always conscious of his plight. The family is suffocation itself.

Again the family in new American Gothic lacks the complexity of the family in the two works mentioned —except perhaps for the fiction of Flannery O'Connor. But the family is immediately shocking: a dying father rolls tennis balls; a boy burns his great-uncle's corpse (or tries to) so that he will not have to bury it; a father forgets the color of his son's eyes; and an adolescent kills the brother he loves.

In an essay on the grotesque William Van O'Connor has written: "Our rational selves want the category, want it fixed and stable. But we also want to recognize the ironic, the paradoxical, the ambiguous, the conflict of equal or almost equal claims. . . . A frequent, possibly an essential, factor in the literature of the grotesque—of the sort that is morally serious, not wilfully monstrous—is that one category erupts inside another category." [6] Mr. O'Connor suggests that the grotesque is produced by disintegration. This disintegration is not only evident in the distortions of narcissism and the family—the two themes described—it is also produced by the technique of new American Gothic. In Gothic, order often breaks down: chronology is confused, identity is blurred, sex is twisted, the buried life erupts. *The total effect is that of a dream.*

Flannery O'Connor has written about *The Lime Twig:* "You suffer *The Lime Twig* like a dream. It seems to be something that is happening to you, that you want to escape from but can't. The reader even has that slight feeling of suffocation that you have when you can't wake up and some evil is being worked on you. This . . . I might have been dreaming myself." [7] That "slight feeling of suffocation" is crucial in new American Gothic. Specific dreams are used to give insights into the buried life and to reinforce the total pattern. Sylvia's situation in "Master Misery" is particularly relevant: she sells her dreams, trying to find some comfort from others. She neglects reality in the process and later is told that she "has had her soul stolen." Her clown-like friend explains the significance of dreams in life (and in Gothic): "But most dreams begin because there are furies inside of us that blow open all the doors. I don't believe in Jesus Christ, but I do believe in people's souls; and I figure it this way, baby: dreams are the mind of the soul and the secret truth about us." "Master Misery" is concerned with more than the selling of dreams; it strives and achieves that slight feeling of suffocation when reality and dream fuse. Capote shows us that Sylvia's categories melt.

Appropriately enough, Miss O'Connor's comments apply to her own fiction. In "The Enduring Chill" she uses the following dream of Asbury Fox:

He went to sleep thinking of the peaceful spot in the family burying ground where he would soon lie, and after a while he saw that his body was being borne slowly toward it while his mother and Mary George [his sister] watched without interest from their chairs on the porch. As the bier was carried across the dam, they could look up and see the procession reflected upside down in the pond. A lean dark figure in a Roman collar followed it. He had a mysteriously saturnine face in which there was a subtle blend of asceticism and corruption.

Obviously, Miss O'Connor is trying to show Asbury's ambivalent feelings toward Catholicism, his mother and sister, and himself. If the dream were eliminated, we would not understand his actions. But the dream strengthens the entire atmosphere: in the story we see "upside-down reflections" everywhere; the "enduring chill" arises from the curious fusion of life and death, reality and unreality.

The dream-like quality of new American Gothic is also established by the "color of darkness." In *63: Dream Palace* we read: "In this section of the park there were no lights, and the only illumination came from the reflection of the traffic blocks away. Here the men who came to wander about as aimless and groping as he were obvious shades in hell." In *The Lime Twig* violence occurs in a steam room: "He crouched and crept down the length of one wall, made his way in blindness and with the floor slats cutting into his feet." The night-journey is presented in *Other Voices, Other Rooms:* "A vine-like latticework of stars frosted the southern sky, and with his eyes he interlinked these spangled vines till he could trace many ice-white resemblances: a steeple, fantastic flowers, a springing cat."

As in nightmares there are haunted houses in Gothic. *Other Voices, Other Rooms* supplies a hint. The "other room" is where the "furies" lie, and it functions metaphorically in many works: the defaced kitchen in *The Member of the Wedding;* the sad café; the dark room in which Private Williams watches Leonora; the apartment of Mrs. H. T. Miller haunted by Miriam; the decadent boarding house in *The Cannibal;* and the house on 63rd Street. New American Gothic uses the haunted castle of old Gothic and sees it as "the final door" through which the ghost-like forces march.

Opposed to the other room is the journey. Characters try to escape to the outside world or return to the room. Again the journey is anxiety-provoking. Thus

Joel Harrison Knox tries to flee from Skulley's Landing; Frankie Addams wants to be a "member of the wedding"; Malcolm leaves the hotel; Mr. and Mrs. Banks go to the horse race; and Hazel Motes wanders into a town to preach the Church Without Christ. All of these journeys end in failure or disaster. Moving is as dangerous as staying at home.

In dreams we often meet a distorted "reflection" of ourselves. People have the wrong heads or bodies. There is a dark stranger we know we have met but we can't remember where. Often these reflections are encountered in new American Gothic. Capote says in *Other Voices, Other Rooms:* "It was as if he lived those months wearing a pair of spectacles with green cracked lenses." In *Ballad of the Sad Café* Miss Amelia's eyes don't focus properly; they are "turned inward so sharply that they seem to be exchanging with each other one long and secret gaze of grief." Another work of Carson McCullers is *Reflections in a Golden Eye.* Seymour Glass has clouded vision; Eloise dislikes the glasses of Ramona in "Uncle Wiggily." New American Gothic presents a world that is decidedly out-of-focus.

Silence is also burdensome. Communication as the bridge between people breaks down. There are mutes in *The Heart Is a Lonely Hunter,* "A Tree of Night," "Raise High the Roof Beam, Carpenters." The Zen *koan* quoted by Salinger is relevant here: "We know the sound of two hands clapping. But what is the sound of one hand clapping?" The writers I discuss try to present "the one hand clapping."

I have dwelt on these recurring metaphors because I think that new American Gothic depends to a great extent on image, not idea. Because it deals with limitations of personality and wars in the family, it seeks not to be expansive but intensive. It presents a vertical world. Perhaps the best way to read Gothic is as "*poetry* of disorder." John W. Aldridge affirms this when he states: "Their novels are as pure, neat, and carefully refined as symbolist poems." [8] Indeed, the highest achievements of new American Gothic are in the story or short novel where the unfolding of the "inmost leaf" is lyrically presented: *The Ballad of the Sad Café, 63: Dream Palace,* "The Headless Hawk," "The Artificial Nigger," "The Laughing Man," and *The Cannibal.* And the best of new American Gothic is an important contribution to modern literature.

2   SELF-LOVE

AT ONE POINT in *Other Voices, Other Rooms* Randolph makes the following observation:

> They can romanticize us so, mirrors, and that is their secret: what a subtle torture it would be to destroy all the mirrors in the world: where then could we look for reassurance of our identities? I tell you, my dear, Narcissus was no egotist . . . he was merely another of us who, in our unshatterable isolation, recognized, on seeing his reflection, the one beautiful comrade, the inseparable love . . . poor Narcissus, possibly the only human who was ever honest on this point.

And Carson McCullers says in *The Ballad of the Sad Café:*

> First of all, love is a joint experience between two persons—but the fact that it is a joint experience does not mean that it is a similar experience to the two people involved. There are the lover and the beloved, but these two come from different countries. Often the beloved is only a stimulus for all the stored up love which has lain quiet within the lover for a long time hitherto. And somehow every lover knows this. He feels in his soul that his love is a solitary thing. He comes to know a new strange loneliness and it is this knowledge that makes him suffer. . . . Let it be added that this lover . . . can be man, woman, child, or indeed any human creature on this earth.

These two observations are true for many characters in new American Gothic. The characters are isolated; they do not and cannot belong to the outside world. This lack of communication creates anxiety. They do not know where to turn for assistance and comfort. Gradually they turn more and more inward (the buried life becomes crucial), and they realize at last that their only "inseparable love" is the mirror. Because they cannot part with the reflection, they compulsively follow Narcissus. The more they love themselves, the less they can escape. Their isolation is complete.

Others approach and create problems. The lovers feel that their narcissistic designs are being destroyed: they resent and want to destroy the others. But at the same time they want to communicate with them, to love them, if only to change them into reflections. (Mrs. McCullers' statement doesn't take this into account.) If the others retain their identities, the lovers lose their security. Usually the cruel ambivalence is resolved only through violence. Conflicts are secretly desired. The lovers can now achieve what they have really wanted; they can jump into the pool and die. Death is the true reflection, offering peace and silence. Ihab Hassan's remark about Mrs. McCullers' fiction can apply to all of new American Gothic; "It would seem that love, in intensifying the lover's pain, in precluding communion, and in electing outlandish recipients, seeks its own impediments." [1]

To return to Randolph. Like Narcissus he is interested in his well-being. He loves his headaches because he can pity himself. He stays in his room, not wanting to see others who are "different." But Randolph is enough of a thinker to realize that the lover at times wants to free himself: he loves others but uses them for his own ends. In the past he loved Dolores:

"Always with her I knew very much that I was alive, and came finally to believe in my own validity." She, however, could not tolerate his love; she knew she was simply a "thing" to give him security. She used all of her energy to defeat him. Randolph then loved (and still loves) Pepe, the fighter, who became the object of her affection. He tried unsuccessfully to attach himself to the power of Pepe, forgetting the other's desires. Narcissism produced violence: Randolph attempted to show his hatred of Pepe by killing him—instead, he shot Ed Sansom, the manager.

The fact that the narcissistic lover is unsure of his role is symbolically presented by Capote. Randolph discovers that the only way he can love his reflection is through masquerade. At a masquerade ball he wears "silver hair and satin slippers, a green mask, [is] wrapped in silk pistachio and pink." He tells us: "at first, before the mirror, this horrifies me, then pleases to rapture, for I am very beautiful." And Randolph must continue to love his secret, beautiful self. He must do more: he must have another person join in the worship. So he makes believe he is the father of Joel; he asks the boy to join him.

Other Capote characters pursue their reflections in less conscious ways than Randolph. Mrs. H. T. Miller in "Miriam" is a good example. Her interests are "narrow," we are told. She has few friends; she rarely leaves her "pleasant" apartment; she is compulsively neat. Like Randolph she is an anxious person who finds that she cannot live alone: she wants to love something. And she discovers Miriam. Miriam, a girl with "silver-white" hair, suddenly appears to take advantage of her: she comes uninvited to the apartment; she takes a brooch; she wants to be kissed good night. In spite of these outrageous actions Mrs. Miller submits to Miriam and even tries to please her with white roses and cakes.

Mrs. Miller is a narcissist who has turned inward so much that she is Miriam. (Note that they both have the same name.) Unable to join the social world, she must love a girlish reflection of herself. This is why she has "a plan of which she had not the least knowledge or control." This is why she acts with "curious passivity." She has retreated so much into the buried life that reality becomes dream-like: "the room was losing shape; it was dark and getting darker and there was nothing to be done about it." Even in retreat the ego of Mrs. Miller tries to assert itself; it refuses to love the destructive urge. Consequently, Mrs. Miller views Miriam as an authoritarian ruler.

Another repressed lover appears in "Master Misery." Sylvia is isolated from the social world (represented by her sister's marriage) that she regards as ugly. She cannot love herself because she is plain-looking. Therefore she is attracted to her dreams: they are exciting. By selling them to Mr. Revercomb, she hopes to earn money and affection: "Mr. Revercomb's lips brushed her ear as he leaned far into her sleep. Tell me? he whispered." Sylvia wants to be desired, even raped, while she recognizes that this narcissistic longing is ultimately destructive. Oreilly, a former seller of dreams, insists that she get her dreams back from Master Misery. He becomes the conscience of Sylvia. (The fact that alcoholic clowning gives him security is neglected by her; he has substituted one kind of self-love for another.) Finally she agrees. Mr. Revercomb informs her that he has *used* her dreams. As a result Sylvia loses Oreilly, her home, and her freedom; she sinks further into herself. "Master Misery" ends with the contemplated rape of Sylvia by two boys; she doesn't care about being attacked because she has "nothing left to steal."

Capote uses the "vicious cycle" as a symbol to show that narcissism lacks progress. Randolph loves Dolores who loves Pepe who is loved by Randolph (but does not love him). Mrs. Miller thinks that like a diver she is emerging "from some deeper, greener depth," but she is sinking into the bottomless pool. Moving and standing still are presented in "Master Misery": "A plaster girl with intense glass eyes sat astride a bicycle pedaling at the maddest pace; though its wheel spokes spun hypnotically, the bicycle of course never bulged." Sylvia is raped by the same two boys she had met a long time ago. In "Shut a Final Door" Walter stares at a fan: "After a while he just lay there in the hot room, shivering, just lay there and watched the slow-turning fan; there was no beginning to its action, and no end; it was a circle." Narcissists cannot break loose from the circle; they cannot even measure it to find the center. Capote does not offer an analysis of the causes of these circular lives. He simply presents them. In "Shut a Final Door" Walter wonders why he is trapped. Has his "churchly" mother, or father, or older sister been responsible? Has *he* been responsible? The questions are never answered. Capote does not allow his narcissists much choice; they are "determined" to be in their circles.

Nonliving images are used to create the perfect atmosphere for compulsive narcissism: Walter is obsessed with the fan and telephone; Miriam plays with a French doll which has an "idiot glass eye"; Vincent in "The Headless Hawk" is cursed by a woman whose voice is a "ragged cut"; "The woman's head [in "A Tree of Night"] snapped up as if she had not been asked a simple question, but stabbed with a needle, too"; Sylvia sees a "life-sized, mechanical" Santa

Claus. Capote is at his best in the opening lines of "Master Misery": "Her high heels, clacking across the marble foyer, made her think of ice cubes rattling in a glass, and the flowers, those autumn chrysanthemums in the urn . . . if touched they would splatter, splinter . . . into frozen dust; yet the house was warm, even somewhat overheated, but cold, and Sylvia shivered, but cold, like the snowy swollen wastes of the secretary's face."

Even natural elements are lifeless: Sylvia sees the flowers as "frozen dust"; in "A Tree of Night" the mute's eyes are like "clouded milky-blue marbles," and his face has a "shocking, embalmed, secret stillness"; Joel Harrison Knox imagines "lilacs bleeding out of the sockets of a skull"; Miriam's fingers make "cobweb movements"; her white hair is "like an albino's"; Walter sleeps with a cripple wearing a "monstrous black shoe"; he thinks at one point that "Christmas trees are cellophane"; and the sky itself is a "thunder-cracked mirror" at the end of "The Headless Hawk."

The characters in Carson McCullers' fiction also suffer from "spiritual isolation" (Oliver Evans' phrase) and narcissism. Perhaps they are more "human" than Capote's because their creator views them with compassion and irony, not simply as automatons. Mr. Evans explains her belief in this respect: "Every individual, she believes, is imprisoned in the cell of his own being, and any practical attempt at communication, such as speech, is doomed to failure." [2] It is more characteristic for her to use natural elements than nonliving ones. In *The Heart Is a Lonely Hunter*, for example, speech is a binding symbol: John Singer cannot sing because he is a mute; although articulate, Doctor Copeland often moans; Jake Blount screams with drunken fury; and Mick wishes that there was some "place where she could go to hum [music] out loud." These characters cannot speak with authority.

The "festive gathering" also breaks down. Frank Baldanza sees the café as a congenial context for conversations in Mrs. McCullers' work, and he notes that violence often explodes in it.[3] Thus in *The Ballad of the Sad Café* Marvin Macy and Cousin Lymon attack Miss Amelia and deface her property. Mr. Baldanza neglects the destructive parties in *The Heart Is a Lonely Hunter*. Mick's first "real" party ends in disaster: "A bunch of girls were running down the street, holding up their dresses and with their hair flying. . . . Some boys had cut off the long, sharp spears of a Spanish bayonet bush and they were chasing the girls with them." Doctor Copeland uses a festive occasion to preach his "strong true purpose." When the four characters go to Singer's room in the climax of the novel, communication falters. In *Reflections in a Golden Eye* the card party is full of tension. There is a ritualistic party for Alison and her houseboy, Anacletto, which *is* enjoyable. Anacletto "had a genius for making some sort of festival out of almost every occasion." Their "very special party" is the last one because Alison dies.

I have stressed the "human" feeling generated by the speech symbol; however, I think it is dangerous to exaggerate the "philosophical" attitudes of Mrs. McCullers and Capote. Frank Baldanza may be right in maintaining that both writers are Platonists who see the "worthlessness of the material realm."[4] For me they present the actions of narcissists more then they do the conflict between real and ideal. Although Mrs. McCullers is a more daring "thinker" than Capote, she also accepts narcissism as a fundamental part of "the human condition." How did people get this way? She doesn't answer. She simply presents them moving in compulsive circles. An elaborate symbol in *The Heart Is a Lonely Hunter* concretizes her belief: "The motionless merry-go-round seemed to Jake like something in a liquor dream. . . . He adjusted a lever and the thin jangle of mechanical music began. The wooden cavalcade around them seemed to cut them off from the rest of the world." The carrousel, like Capote's circle, symbolizes the isolation of narcissists from the "rest of the world."

In *The Heart Is a Lonely Hunter* the four major characters (excluding Singer) are narcissistic, even though they do not realize it. Blount maintains that he is a builder of the future. He believes wholeheartedly in Marxism, wandering from town to town to preach its gospel. But Blount has adopted his "social truths" to ward off thinking about his defects. He has done more: by using Marxism to assert his superior intelligence, he fights anxiety. Blount, in other words, is ambivalent: he wants peace but uses violence; he loathes and loves power. His Marxism is his one truth and, like Anderson's characters, it makes him grotesque.

Dr. Copeland also believes in justice, proclaiming equality for the Negro. He is a compulsive follower of his strong true purpose because it helps him to refrain from questioning what he has done to himself and his children. Copeland is another Hollingsworth who falls in love with abstractionism—to the exclusion of anything else. Portia, his daughter, tells him: "A person can't pick up they children and just squeeze them to which-a-way they wants them to be. Whether it hurt them or not. Whether it right or wrong." Mrs. McCullers, unlike Capote, understands that narcissism is tied to social reform. Ihab Hassan writes: "Through Copeland and Blount, the novel gains its force of social reference; the idea of fascism abroad is constantly played off against that of racism at home." [5] The point the novel makes is stronger: in their narcissistic will to power men manipulate social truths.

Unlike the two "humanitarians," Mick Kelley acknowledges her need to help herself. As any adolescent she loves herself; she cannot really think of the rest of the world. At the same time she wants to move from her "inner room" (where music and Singer reside) to the outside room. She does learn partially about the limitations of her father; she does understand more about sex. Mick can never relate the two worlds and, although she gets a job at the Woolworth store, she retreats into her inner room where she can still gain some pleasure.

Biff tries to feel affection for others: for Mick, Blount, and his dead wife, Alice. He even keeps his café open all night for strangers. These desperate efforts conflict with his narcissism. Two things show us Biff's self-centeredness: he likes "freaks" and he is bisexual. Mrs. McCullers tells us that he had a "special friendly feeling for sick people and cripples." He sees himself in them; he does not accept them for what they are. At one point he thinks: "By nature all people are both sexes." Subconsciously Biff knows that his two-sided nature alienates him from men and women; again he projects his disturbance on others. The ambivalence is never resolved: "Between the two worlds he was suspended."

Mrs. McCullers has given us four narcissists who reflect one another (Mick-Biff, Blount-Copeland) and yet cannot see the similarities they have.[6] This accounts for the irony of the novel. The irony is complicated by the projection of their narcissism onto Singer. Singer is like Moby Dick. His muteness is "white." People read meanings into both nonreflecting images. "Each man described the mute as he wished him to be" in the way each man sees himself in the whale.

Like Ahab the four characters take advantage of the blank tablet. Afraid to live their secret desires, more afraid to admit them to others, they find a solution in Singer as mirror: "Because in some men it is in them to give up everything personal at some time, before it ferments and poisons—throw it to some human being or human idea." The four, by talking to Singer, pretend that they are outgoing and therefore relieve themselves of guilt. All seek the mute because they seek themselves. Copeland, for example, sees Singer as "oppressed"; Mick thinks he hears secret music. Meanwhile Singer as a person is forgotten and destroyed. This is why he is a Christ-figure. Singer is caught because he is loved by them and he loves Antonapoulos. The Greek functions as a kind of mirror-image of the four: he is also narcissistic, caring more for self-satisfaction than for Singer. Where is the mute to turn? Mrs. McCullers offers one further irony. Singer is not a true lover of others: if he did understand and love the four people who desperately need him, he would not commit suicide. Singer's final act is narcissistic. By suicide, he asserts that he loves himself so much that he can destroy this love. He wills himself to power. In this respect he becomes a false Christ.

In *Reflections in a Golden Eye* we meet many more narcissists. Leonora Penderton, a bit feebleminded, loves her body and prances naked through the living room; Alison loves her illness; Private Williams is so withdrawn that he walks in a "trance"; and the Major delights in his wit and adultery. All are more inhuman than the people we meet in *The Heart Is a Lonely Hunter*, largely as a result of insistent imagery.

The atmosphere is established in the first paragraph. We are told that the army post is "designed according to a certain rigid pattern." The things that happen there "happen over and over again." This rigidity is reflected in the compulsive actions of the characters. Even violence which breaks the routine is wild as in the case of Williams, who has the "eyes of animals." Mrs. McCullers stresses the rigidity and the violence (the two are linked) throughout the novelette. All of the repetitious actions are either compulsive or wild. Captain Penderton, for example, is said to have done this:

> He had driven into a town near the post where he was then stationed, had parked his car, and walked for a long time in the streets. In the course of this walk the Captain came upon a tiny kitten hovered in a doorway. . . . For a long time he looked into the soft, gentle little face and stroked the warm fur. . . . At last the Captain had taken the kitten with him down the street. On the corner there was a mailbox and after one quick glance around him he had opened the freezing letter slot and squeezed the kitten inside.

The incident is important: the "living" is squeezed into the "mechanical"; the Captain *repeats* his action at the end of the novel when he attacks Private Williams. In an even more brutal incident Alison cuts off her nipples with garden shears. Penderton takes a Seconal and feels a "great dark bird alighted on his chest." All three examples show the living threatened by the nonliving. How appropriate in a novel that emphasizes narcissistic compulsion!

Captain Penderton is the hero of the novelette. Like Randolph and Biff he is suspended between two worlds: he "obtained within himself a delicate balance between the male and the female elements"; he loves death more than life. The Captain is a coward, and his awareness of this fact plagues him. Plagues him, yet fascinates him. Mrs. McCullers also introduces the abstractionism I have noted in Hollingsworth, Ahab, and Dr. Copeland. The Captain's head is "filled with statistics"; he has the "knowledge of many separate facts." Abstractions or statistics are impersonal. Penderton becomes nonliving as he submits to his compulsive routine, but he cannot leave it. He loves it even more than his troubles. Indeed, Penderton looks upon his delicate balance as an interesting "fact."

His compulsive design grows. He looks at his environment in the same clinical way because that is the only way he can understand and be equal to it. Mrs. McCullers introduces Private Williams as a perfect love-and-hate object for the Captain. Because Williams is wild and instinctive he annoys Penderton who must make him into fact. An early passage sets the tone of the relationship. The Captain instructs Williams to clear the lawn as far as the oak tree—symbolically, to conform to his pattern. However, the other instinctively "ruins" everything when he cuts the tree. The rest of the novelette shows the inevitable effect of compulsion upon the "natural man," "a dark, drugged craving as certain of fulfillment as death."

In his preparation for the final embrace with Williams, the Captain sets out to tame wild nature in the horse, Firebird. Two things are crucial to the ride: Penderton tries to check the freedom of Firebird by starting and stopping abruptly, but he loses to the horse. The natural world bursts into his consciousness and he has a mystical vision: the "world was a kaleidoscope." His attack on Williams (who silently observes Leonora sleeping) is sudden—that is, Penderton again slips from compulsion into wildness. Although he has prepared for the end, it is unexpected. He shoots Williams without thinking. In spite of the fact that Penderton gives way, he does make Williams into a fact and assures *his* own death as well.

Miss Amelia in *The Ballad of the Sad Café* is at first

a narcissist who likes to exert her power over others: "The only use that Miss Amelia had for other people was to make money out of them." She uses her schemes to fool and tame them. Like the Captain Miss Amelia is a creature of fact, but she wants to get away from herself. Lymon, like Williams, is "funny"—he cannot fit into the pattern. Miss Amelia, however, sees her "freakishness" in the hunchback. By loving him she can love herself a bit more. Mrs. McCullers describes the one "great, twisted shadow of the two of them." Ironically enough, "Cousin" Lymon is also self-centered. He capitalizes on Miss Amelia's desperate love and uses her more than she does him. He gets what he wants: clothing, food, and great self-importance. These ironies are compounded. Marvin Macy, the former husband of Miss Amelia, returns to town to gain vengeance. He battles with her and, as he is about to lose, Cousin Lymon jumps onto her back, and he and Macy run away after defacing the property. The circle again asserts itself.

Mrs. McCullers has described the relationship of the lover to beloved in this way: "For the lover is forever trying to strip bare his beloved. The lover craves any possible relation with his beloved, even if this experience can cause him only pain." Why should this be? I have suggested that her lovers are narcissists who want their love-objects to mirror themselves. But because the loved are alive, they cannot bear being reflections. Often they too are narcissists. They rebel violently. Furthermore, Mrs. McCullers seems to suggest that each person is both lover and beloved of himself. The horrifying relationships of Penderton and Williams, Miss Amelia and Lymon, are the seeds everyone carries in his buried life.

There is an easy transition from Mrs. McCullers' lovers to those of Salinger. In his fiction we meet strangers who want to communicate with others but withdraw into the inner room and gradually like living there. Eloise in "Uncle Wiggily in Connecticut" is anxious: she cannot find fulfillment in her marriage; she dislikes Connecticut. For a time she finds some kind of outlet in compulsive talking and drinking. In her own household, however, lurks Ramona, her child. Because the girl is lonely and ugly, she invents friendships with "Jimmy Jimmereeno" and, later, with "Mickey Mickeranno." Eloise is always reminded of her wounds when she looks at Ramona: she remembers her own boy friends before her present unsuccessful marriage, and she recalls Walt, her favorite.

Two incidents in which he is involved are remembered. The first is running for the bus with him, falling suddenly, and twisting her ankle. Walt referred to her injured ankle as "Poor Uncle Wiggily." This incident is related in Eloise's mind to the war wounds and the death of her favorite. Eloise realizes in her tipsy way that she has not defined her self; her memories are more meaningful than her Connecticut friends.

Salinger demonstrates that her anxiety becomes narcissistic and destructive. Eloise discovers her daughter lying in bed next to another invisible friend. She screams at her to awake, realizing that as a child Ramona can substitute a live "Mickey Mickeranno" for a dead "Jimmy Jimmereeno," and be happy sleeping next to him. She forces her to lie in the center of the bed, frustrating the fantasy, because she resents the child's innocence. Eloise returns to the living room, afraid to live as an injured Uncle Wiggily. But she has the strength only to retreat into her adolescence. Like Mrs. H. T. Miller she falls in love with her youthful reflection.

"Uncle Wiggily in Connecticut" is a typical early Salinger story. Eloise's world is social, "all-American," but fantasy intrudes in the midst of it. Perhaps Salinger's Gothic is more horrifying than that of Capote and Mrs. McCullers because of the tension of almost diametrically opposed social reality and private fantasy. This is especially evident in "The Laughing Man." Here the hero, or at least the important adult, is the Chief, a law student at NYU, who lives with the children more easily than he does with adults. We see him through the eyes of the child-narrator. The narrator accepts the Chief as a great man—he takes him and his gang on trips, and, what is important, he tells them stories about the Laughing Man. The Chief-Laughing Man equation is crucial. We learn that the Chief is lonely and ugly, that his fictional hero, having these characteristics is glamorized—the Laughing Man is kept away from the world by bandits who have deformed his face (another symbolic injury). Salinger concentrates upon the "pale-red gossamer mask out of poppy petals" worn by the Laughing Man. I take the mask to be symbolic. The Chief is actually wearing a mask when he tells these stories; the mask hides his insufficient self and makes him heroic through fantasy. He loves his glamorized reflection.

The Chief's retreat into fantasy is opposed to his relationship with Mary. We feel that not loving him, she meets him only when she visits the dentist. When Mary leaves him, after refusing to play baseball with the kids, the narrator does not understand the meaning of the affair. He does sense something is wrong as he hears the last installment of the Laughing Man cycle. The Chief has been hurt by reality; consequently his story is concerned with the destruction of his reflection. The Laughing Man is shot by his arch-enemies, the Dufarges, and he dies in the forest, close to the animals he had once befriended. Salinger seems to imply that the Chief can now live only with a knowledge of inferiority. The Chief will probably retreat more into fantasy and never return to Central Park.

Opposed to Eloise and the Chief are the mystical lovers. Although Salinger seems to imply that the latter are capable of loving the universe (they are so expansive!) they are actually rose-colored fantasists. Teddy, for example, is a boy genius who denies self. Everything merges into a Zen One. It is always difficult to discover the causes of belief, especially religious belief, but I think we should try to see some psychological causes at work here.

Teddy seems to accept his philosophy because it helps him to escape from anxiety. Being divine, he does not have to face love and hate (or any ambivalence); he does not, in other words, have to risk self-definition. Where does *he* begin or end? Teddy refuses to answer the question (it does not "exist") because no thing "stops off somewhere." He embraces the universe: his mysticism is a monstrous kind of self-love. Teddy is like Whitman. Whitman loved himself as he loved God. In fact, he was so fond of himself that he thought he was God. Teddy also resembles the poet in his longing for death. Death presumably does not "stop."

"Teddy" may be a mystical story for Salinger, but I think it is Gothic. It shows us that narcissism generates divinity. Most of Salinger's later stories are similar in the complete tension between Gothic and mysticism. "Franny" deals with a frustrated person who is sick of ego. Like Teddy she is intent upon withdrawal from the self and fusion with the One. Her description of the meditative way stresses the loss of all personal devices and social impingements. The word, "God," should be repeated until it comes, as it were, by itself. The process again embodies a retreat from society and individuality (although magnified self-love is present);

mystically it is an exploration of infinity. Salinger uses the public washroom as a setting for Franny's introspection. For me the tile has the symbolic value of infinity, of the absence of the individual. What is surrealistic is the fact that the washroom would usually be considered public. Salinger has purposefully omitted most of the other people and concentrated upon the *tile*. In a related way he tries to communicate Franny's vision (this is what we must call it) through a suggestion of unheard words. The question is: Are the words soundless to people afflicted with self-love? Can Franny hear the words because she knows more than they will ever know? Or, are the words representative of a narcissist talking to herself? Salinger views Franny as a representative "spirit" in materialistic society. Perhaps she has withdrawn so much that she generates false divinity.

Seymour Glass is the crucial lover. Before discussing "Raise High the Roof Beam, Carpenters," I want to look at the earlier "A Perfect Day for Bananafish." Seymour cannot forget the war; we are told that he has had a nervous breakdown. His wife, Muriel, is too interested in a vacation at the Florida resort to worry about Seymour's health. Salinger describes the social climate at length before we actually see the hero, and this is fitting—he wants us to condemn Muriel, her mother (to whom she is speaking on the phone), and their materialistic views. He tries to satirize the reality with which Seymour has to cope.

Then Salinger changes the setting. We emerge into fresh air and come face to face with Sybil, a child fond of Seymour. Her mother doesn't understand when she murmurs: "See more glass." Sybil's mother and Muriel are related because both cannot discover meanings in anything seemingly full of nonsense. They are "rational" adults. Thus an alliance between the child-

hood world and the maladjusted self is suggested. We
see Seymour at last, visibly isolated and pale. He and
Sybil proceed to jump into the water, and we learn
about the bananafish. Seymour's bananafish represents
his creative self, longing to complete his individuality
and manhood. The self, however, seems to be doomed
because it cannot differentiate between kinds of experience; it is a glutton. Seymour wants to love everyone, but he cannot separate this love from self-love.
Painful irresolution causes his suicide. Narcissus
drowns.

In "Raise High the Roof Beam, Carpenters" Salinger returns to Seymour, trying to understand him fully.
He is careful not to make the hero appear in the story
except through his diary entries. This technique is better than the one in "Teddy." We respond to Seymour
and what he represents more easily than we do to the
boy genius—he is less didactic and more "normal."
Salinger has also used the narrator, the brother of the
hero, as an involved, average spokesman; his normality
strengthens the reaction Seymour forces upon him and,
consequently, upon us. We feel, in other words, that
the hero is to be understood as seriously as his brother
understands him.

Again the device of the wedding party, like the week-
end in "Franny," brings superficial, sophisticated society into focus, and counterposes it to Seymour, who
is confused about marriage, and does not attend his
own wedding. The Matron of Honor expresses the
general view when she says that Seymour had never
learned to relate to anybody. The relatives, it appears,
are less interested in Seymour than in their own views.
One of them, however, doesn't say anything at all—
he is a deaf-mute. When asked on paper if he wants to
have a drink after the car has been blocked by a pa-
rade, he writes "Delighted." Salinger takes the group of

six to the narrator's apartment, where most of them continue speaking about Seymour's inadequacies.

Salinger has explored the narcissism of the people who oppose the hero. Seymour cannot answer directly; the narrator, however, discovers his brother's diary and removes it from sight. He decides to read it in the bathroom. In the diary Seymour explains his confused philosophy. He is aware of the beautiful in all things. As a child he throws a stone at a girl because he wants to express his love. Later he calls Muriel "noble." The bananafish in him responds to the beautiful without discrimination—that is, he cannot distinguish other possible, nonbeautiful meanings. And he cannot see that his bountiful embrace is an attempt to forget anxiety. Seymour reveals unconsciously that he is a river without boundaries.

Which leads us to the deaf-mute. He symbolizes a great degree of self-knowledge and social commitment. He sees things as beautifully *related*; Seymour sees things as beautifully *isolated*. The mute knows how to love; he is at peace with all aspects of reality. I think that like John Singer, he is given too much credit by the narrator who hopes that as an Ideal he can teach Seymour to be a proper lover. Salinger does not characterize the mute; he can merely describe him as he desires him. The mute is an abstraction, not a person.

The confusion in Salinger's later stories indicates that he has not been true to his Gothic muse: he has neglected anxiety for mysticism. But the narcissism of the early stories is still present, asserting itself as divinity. Flannery O'Connor has written: "My own feeling is that writers who see by the Christian faith will have, in these times, the sharpest eyes for the grotesque, for the perverse, and for the unacceptable." [7] Using Catholicism as a "vantage point in the universe," she views "displaced persons" who have adopted one truth: the "rejection of the Scheme of Redemption." [8] Narcissism is given an explicit theological framework. Substituting self-love for love of Christ, Miss O'Connor's grotesques are "lost in that abyss which opens for man when he sets up as God." [9] This is not to say that they do not suffer from the same mental illness that Randolph, Captain Penderton and Eloise have—they are also anxious, compulsive, and malicious.

Actually the Christ-figure, although prominent in Miss O'Connor's fiction, plays a significant part in new American Gothic. Non-Catholic writers can use him because of his obvious pertinence: in a dramatic way he opposes the narcissist. He is not anxious; he is flexible; and he loves all. John Singer assumes the role: he holds all meanings others attach to him. Early in the novel Alice, Biff's wife, reads a passage from the New Testament: "And when they had found Him, they said unto Him, 'All men seek for Thee.'" Mrs. McCullers ironically suggests that Biff, Blount, Copeland, and Mick becomes Singer's disciples—they are all Judas-figures. As Biff says, they have to "throw" their ideas onto him. Singer is crucified because he "heard things nobody else had ever heard." Not a Catholic, Mrs. McCullers' Christ is tinged with self-love: he kills himself.

The mixture of awe and irony in Singer's portrayal is evident in Salinger's portrayal of the Christ-like Seymour Glass. Seymour tries to see the beautiful in all things, but he is crucified by a selfish world. The undercurrent of Christian symbolism in "Raise High the Roof Beam, Carpenters" rises to the surface in "Zooey." Zooey tells his sister, Franny, who is tempted by self-interest, that Seymour, their brother, used to make them shine their shoes before they appeared on the radio quiz program. Seymour said they

were to play for the Fat Lady. Zooey comments: The
Fat Lady is Christ Himself. Christ in Salinger's story
is everyone: universal love is necessary.

Even in Capote's "Master Misery" we see the need
of the narcissist to "confess." Sylvia's relationship
with Mr. Revercomb is parallel in a way to the relationships already noted. Because she has only her
dreams to sell, she tries to use them to gain comforting
guidance from Master Misery. She sees him as an all-
embracing lover. Can he be an ironic inversion of the
Christ-figure? Remember that dreams are, as Oreilly
says, "the mind of the soul." Capote may not, like
Oreilly, believe in Jesus Christ, but he sees him darkly
in "Master Misery."

As a Catholic Miss O'Connor does believe in the
divinity of Christ; she cannot say that He is a Fat
Lady as can Zooey or that He is suicidal. But she can
show that a narcissist views himself as a new prophet.
Hazel Motes is a clouded Christ. Hazel, the hero of
Wise Blood, is a religious fanatic. The one "truth"
that he preaches in rooming houses and on street
corners is: "Nothing matters but that Jesus don't
exist." He assumes that he is more meaningful than
Jesus. Hazel cannot abandon his faith because it mirrors his self-love; by believing that he *matters*, not
Jesus, he lashes out at his mother's orthodoxy and the
anxiety it generated in him. The more converts he
gains for his Church Without Christ, the more power
he will have. Hazel is caught in a compulsive circle.

Because Hazel has adopted a life of grotesque abstractionism (like Penderton or Dr. Copeland), Miss
O'Connor stresses imagistically his mechanized existence: "His black hat sat on his head with a careful,
placed expression and his face had a fragile look as if
it had been broken and stuck together again, or like a
gun no one knows is loaded." He is always on edge: he

sits "at a forward angle on the green plush seat, looking one minute at the window as if he might want to jump out of it." Something in him wants to break loose: his "heart began to grip him like a little ape clutching the bars of its cage."

Miss O'Connor does more than use such imagery to indicate Hazel's lack of humanity. She introduces Enoch Emory as a grotesque reflection of the already grotesque preacher. Enoch claims compulsively that he has "wise blood"; he has submitted to this blood and he waits for its commands: "His blood all morning had been saying the person would come today." The wise blood of Enoch tells him to obey the teachings of Hazel. Leader and led are bound. Enoch has a mission in life: by stealing the mummy from the museum, he can supply a "new jesus" to the Church Without Christ. Furthermore, he can feel that he is a true disciple. Why does Miss O'Connor introduce the mummy? Both Enoch and Hazel have become lifeless automatons.

Wise Blood uses the circle as a crucial symbol. Although Hazel has based his entire life on the assumption that Jesus doesn't exist, he himself begins to be Christ-like. After he kills Layfield (a true believer) he is compelled to listen to the last words. These move him so much that he places barbed wire around his wrist. Later he blinds himself. Hazel Motes loses his self-love when he sees others suffer for the Truth. He becomes the "pin point of light." Again the tension between Gothic and mysticism rises to the surface. *Wise Blood* like "Teddy" seems to be balancing unsuccessfully two opposing ideas. We wonder: Is Hazel truly Christ-like at the end? Or is his conversion simply another aspect of his compulsive, self-destructive narcissism? Is Miss O'Connor giving us false grotesque?

In "A Good Man Is Hard to Find" the Misfit is the same kind of fanatic as Hazel Motes. He also believes that things would be different if Jesus had really done what He said: "He thrown everything off balance. If He did what he said, then it's nothing for you to do but throw away everything and follow Him, and if He didn't, then it's nothing for you to do but enjoy the few minutes you got left the best way you can—by killing somebody or burning down his house or some other meanness to him. No pleasure but meanness." The Misfit's anxiety is always present, but he fights it by means of self-love. Making his life one of pleasure-giving "meanness," he rights the "balance." He becomes a new Jesus. All the time, however, he realizes that "it's no real pleasure in life."

The grandmother is a foil to the Misfit. She is, no doubt, considered a good person by the community. But she is also "mean": she forces her family to obey her; she sees them as an extension of herself. Miss O'Connor writes: "The grandmother didn't want to go to Florida. She wanted to visit some of her connections in east Tennessee and she was seizing at every chance to change Bailey's mind." Later the grandmother delights in her attire—"anyone seeing her dead on the highway would know at once that she was a lady"—and her knowledge of the countryside. She convinces her son to turn the car in the direction of the house with the "secret panel," causing them to meet the Misfit. She seals the death of the family.

Many critics have commented on Miss O'Connor's irony, but they have not explained why it is so devastating. Her irony lies in an awareness that all people—criminal and grandmother—are in love with themselves. "Good country people" express their self-love in gossip, criminals in brutality. When two displaced persons meet, violence occurs. Society, built on imperfect standards of self-love, refuses to acknowledge universal narcissism: it casts the label "bad" on criminals—that is, on people whose narcissism erupts.

The juxtaposition of criminal and lady is evident in "Good Country People." Hulga (formerly Joy) delights in her ugliness and intelligence. By an "act of will" she loves her brooding, skeptical conception of the world. Her "constant outrage had obliterated every expression from her face," but it gives her "pleasure." Hulga's rigid abstractionism resembles that of Penderton and Doctor Copeland—the good country people are for her mere fact. Her artificial leg symbolizes this crippled view. The Bible salesman Miss O'Connor introduces is frightening to Hulga: he seems so happy, believing in all the things she cannot. Hulga decides to hurt him to regain her cruel certainty; she plans to seduce him. But the Bible salesman turns out to be a criminal who seduces her so that he can add her leg to his collection. Hulga allows him to, because she likes being worshipped. The end of the story is startling: the Bible salesman flees after admitting that he too believes in nothing (except his own pleasure). Hulga is left without her wooden support. She can no longer use the world; it uses her.

In "The Displaced Person" Mrs. Shortley, considerably less intelligent than Hulga, is so narcissistic that she considers herself a ruler of the community (she and her family are tenant farmers). She is pictured as the "giant wife of the countryside." She has the "grand self-confidence of a mountain." Her granite nature does not allow her to see the D.P., Mr. Guizac, and his family as more than demonical intruders or "rats with typhoid fleas." Miss O'Connor does not spare irony: Mrs. Shortley compares his children to her own, and finds that, as expected, her own are better.

Mrs. Shortley tries to inform Mrs. McIntyre (en-

tire?) that she must send the D.P.'s away, but the
proprietor does not obey. Pleased by the Pole's effi-
ciency in contrast to Mr. Shortley's laziness, she dis-
places the Shortleys. Then the characteristic pattern
emerges: Mrs. McIntyre, left alone without her gos-
siping reflection, becomes anxious. She turns upon Mr.
Guizac because he represents an alien way of life, one
which threatens her self-centered pleasure. After Mr.
Shortley returns with the news of his wife's death—
the D.P. "killed her"—Mrs. McIntyre rushes to tell
Mr. Guizac to leave. Before she can notify him, he is
crushed to death by Mr. Shortley's tractor. Knowing
that her narcissistic pleasure has helped in the sacrifice,
she goes into a trance: "She felt she was in some foreign country."

"The Displaced Person" is in one way like *The
Heart Is a Lonely Hunter*. Miss O'Connor binds narcissism to social forces: the lovers, Mrs. Shortley and
Mrs. McIntyre (and the Negroes), are "frozen in col-
lusion forever." Their community takes advantage of
—and kills—the person who does not fit. (The fact
that Mr. Guizac speaks a strange language makes him
resemble Singer.) Louis D. Rubin's point about "The
Displaced Person" can also apply to the novel: "They
are in Eden, but the evil of our time impinges. When it
comes, they are helpless, unprepared, and would deny
it and reaffirm their innocence. They cannot do so, and
they are destroyed." [10] I have suggested that their "innocence" is narcissistic.

Unlike the other writers already discussed, John
Hawkes has not received recognition for his Gothic
talent. Perhaps he is less popular because his fiction appears completely out-of-focus. He prefers to present
characters who "float in a space where essence is in-
distinctness, endure in a time which refuses either to
begin or end." [11] What is at the center of his "con-

junction of reason and madness, blur and focus"? [12]
One of the chief concerns of Hawkes is narcissism. In
The Cannibal he presents an overwhelming study of
Germany in 1914 and 1945. Like Mrs. McCullers and
Miss O'Connor he shows us that the community is
often a monstrous reflection of individual lovers. The
narrator is Zizendorf. Zizendorf resembles the others
who have neglected everything except one abstraction: he must kill the American soldier who guards
his sector. His mission, he proclaims, is based on love
of the fatherland: "The rise of the German people and
their reconstruction is no longer questionable—the
land, the Teutonic land, gives birth to the strongest of
races, the Teutonic race." But Hawkes shows us that
underneath Zizendorf's will to power is great anxiety.
The German asserts leadership because he needs adu-
lation and respect which will enhance his self-love. He
plays a role; the other weaklings around him believe in
the grotesque illusion: they become loyal followers.
"Success is almost ours." Ironically enough, Zizendorf's victim, Leevey, is also self-centered. He likes
being "overseer for a sector of land that was one-third
of the nation," although he "frowns with the responsibility." The American reflects his German counterpart
in neglecting common humanity. He simply regards
Germans as instruments to be manipulated—like the
slut he uses.

The title of the novel refers, then, to the narcissistic
cannibalism that eats the community. Hawkes, however, introduces an actual cannibal who, like Enoch
Emory, exaggerates the already grotesque situation.
The Duke pursues a boy, slashes him, and takes the
fragments to his house for dinner. His inhumanity is
pictured in the following way: "The very fact that it
was not a deer or a possum made the thing hard to
skin . . . ; its infernal humanness carried over even in

death and made the carcass just as difficult as the human being had itself been. Every time a bone broke his prize became mangled, every piece that was lost in the mud made the whole thing defective, more imperfect in death." The Duke believes in ordered perfection. By seeking this perfection (which is never achieved) he loses his humanity: *he* becomes "mangled" and "defective."

I have suggested that a recurrent image in new American Gothic is the "mechanical." Hawkes suggests the horror of Germany by using almost obsessively such imagery. We have seen the methodical cannibalism of the Duke. Akin to it is the insistence on the institution. In the very first sentence we see "its delicate and isolated buildings trembling over the gravel and cinder floor of the valley." The institution opens at the end of the novel when "public spirit" revives it. The insane asylum—like the rigid army camp of Mrs. McCullers—is a proper setting for narcissistic compulsion. The entire landscape of *The Cannibal* is cluttered with metallic, nonhuman elements: hatchets, motorcycles, and steel canes.

Animals emerge to engulf humanity. We read: "The town . . . was as shriveled in structure and as decomposed as an oxen's tongue black with ants." Food is unappetizing: "sleek" sausages "bulged like pig's hind legs." Dogs pursue the train: "these dogs ran with the train, nipped at the tie rods, snapped at the lantern from the caboose, and carrying on conversation with the running wheels, begged to be let into the common parlor." The Merchant's corpse is pictured: "in his open mouth there rested a large cacoon, vividly protruding and white, which moved sometimes as if it were alive." The emphasis on the animalistic and the mechanical influences our attitude toward the characters. Hawkes presents an inhuman world in which people are trapped; they cannot rise above what Albert J. Guerard calls "impotent mechanical ruttings." [13] They are Bosch-like creatures.

Hawkes also uses animalistic imagery in *The Owl*. Here the hangman of a strangely medieval town is viewed as the owl. History has decreed that his escutcheon bear the bird: "with wisdom, horns, and field rodent half-destroyed, hardly visible under the talons." He falls in love with the dynastic role, and he always acts like a cruel bird. He preys on the weak community under his mountain-top castle. A Zizendorf, he drowns in his reflection as he "assumed rule to the archaic slow drumming of the nocturnal thick wings . . . bearing instantaneously the pain of authority."

As in *The Cannibal* stone and metal replace the human element. Thus we are given a lengthy description of the castle which images the "iron-edged view of the world" possessed by its master. Even the ritual hanging emphasizes "chains" and "bolts" for the victim. (Actually there are two victims: the hangman and the hanged.) The vital sun is "urged down the spires of the scaffold." The landscape is dominated by the "power of blackness." The hangman's black hood symbolizes his refusal to see humanity clearly; he prefers to recognize weakness, sin, guilt. But the people who live under his rule are attracted to the hood—"all their thoughts and feelings, the very grayness of hair, vanished when the hangman put on his black cape." The hangman watches the "coming of dark from the high tower."

In this inhuman, suffocating, iron world Hawkes introduces Antonia. Because the hangman delights in attacking the "normal," the living, he loves the girl. He refuses to allow her to marry the prisoner. He uses her as does Leevey the slut to consolidate his power. Antonia, attracted and repelled like all of the citizens, succumbs to him and consequently loses her chance for marriage and health. At the end of the novelette, we see Antonia with "altered" complexion: "the rest of her days would be spent with the manual for the virgins not yet released to marriage."

The Owl stresses the "covenant" between hangman and hanged, lover and loved, in a metaphoric way. It could have been a much greater work if Hawkes had made us understand why the narcissistic urge erupts. As do Capote and Mrs. McCullers he presents a stylized closed circle or—to use his words—a "demon's iron halo." But why do some love their halo? And how did they get it?

The Lime Twig, Hawkes' latest novel, presents the same theme: the inhuman reflection of narcissism. Leslie Fiedler has defined it as "the fact that love breeding terror is itself the final terror." [14] The first lover we meet is Hencher. A weak son who lives with his mother, he can never grow up. He likes the security she offers him (even when he is middle-aged). Never able to separate himself from her while she is alive, he must continue to live with her after death. He returns to the old rooming house; he eats the same food. He falls in love with "past glory" but it is evident that he really loves his sick, effeminate nature. It is all he has. Hencher lives a circular, compulsive life. He circles back to the rooming house where he lived with his mother. He "prowls" through the apartment: "I found her [Margaret's] small tube of cosmetic for the lips and, in the lavatory, drew a red circle with it round each of my eyes." Earlier he enters an airplane which has crashed and settles the pilot's "helmet securely on his own smooth head." He returns always to the womb.

His circular life drowns Mr. and Mrs. Banks. Because of his own dream-like state, Banks submits to Hencher's crazy plea to steal a horse. By doing so, he can become his unreal, glamorized reflection—that of sportsman and lover. Banks flees from "suffocating" marriage to the race track—another violent circle. Mrs. Banks also lives in a fragmented world. She cannot live without her husband. The love is too unnatural to remain intact. Margaret is a child: the only way she can exist is by becoming her husband (as Hencher becomes his mother). She waits patiently for him to return; she becomes "dead to the world."

Responsible for the tragedies—Hencher is kicked to death by the horse; Margaret is beaten by one thief; Michael falls onto the track before the field of horses —are thieves. Hawkes shows us that they are narcissists who will themselves to power. Larry is in charge. He cares only about himself, using weaklings to help him assert power. (As in *The Owl* and *The Cannibal* slave and master are two sides of the same coin.) In spite of overwhelming pride, Larry is as compulsive and dream-like as Hencher and Michael Banks. He must have Little Dora and the others idolize him: "Larry turned slowly round so they could see, and there was the gun's blue butt, the dazzling links of steel, the hairless and swarthy torso."

Again Hawkes uses the mechanical to reinforce the inhuman compulsion of narcissists. Note the "dazzling links of steel" mentioned above. The entire existence of Larry is dominated by steel or stone. When we first see him, he is described as "heavy as a horse cart of stone." Later we see his "vest of linked steel, shiny, weighing about five pounds." There is repeated emphasis on material (as in *The Cannibal*). Margaret becomes a "white sheet"; Hencher wears elastic sleeves on his thighs; the thieves cut the "stuffing in bulky sawdust layers away from the frame of the furniture."

In this nonliving world action is either violent or automatic (often both): in the steam room we see "only a lower world of turning and crawling and drowning men." Michael Banks "pumps the hand" of Syb, his dancing partner. Thick's arm "quivers" as he pounds Margaret with the "truncheon." The "riders coming knee to knee with tangle of sticks and the noise" kill Banks. Leslie Fiedler is surely correct when he states that Hawkes gives us the "consciousness we live by but do not record in books—untidy, half-focused, disarrayed." [15] At the center of this consciousness lies the pool of Narcissus.

Turning to the world James Purdy gives us, we encounter what Edith Sitwell has called the "suffering, blundering cruelty of love." [16] The hero of a Purdy story is a misfit who, thrown back upon his own resources, is afraid to live with himself and more afraid to leave himself. He wants to escape from the pool of Narcissus but cannot. Eventually he drowns. I do not mean to imply that Purdy is the same kind of stylist as Hawkes. His style is natural, clear, and "reasonable." Imagery of metal or cloth does not abound. Time is not destroyed. Perhaps he resembles Salinger more than any of the Gothic writers: like him he depends largely on everyday dialogue, very little on description. His heroes are, for the most part, people we see on the bus or at work; odd—but not *very* odd—things lurk in their "normal" worlds. And these things grow in size until they break down order.

Thus "Color of Darkness" begins in a matter-of-fact way: "Sometimes he thought about his wife, but a thing had begun of late, usually after the boy went to bed, a thing which *should* have been terrifying but which was not: he could not remember now what she had looked like." Note the calm, reflective nature of the hero: even a possibly terrifying thing cannot disturb him; note the smallness of the thing: the color of eyes. We are a long way from the owl or the cannibal. But Purdy's hero is also narcissistic. Gradually he realizes that he cannot even remember the color of his son's eyes or those of Mrs. Zilke's. And he tries to excuse himself: "You know," he said, confidentially, "when you have just your work as I do, people get away from you." The "just" is crucial. The hero has given his life to his work and has lost his humanity, his memory. Because he—like Eloise—sees his son before him, he cannot keep excusing himself. He must acknowledge kinship.

Purdy's symbols are always clear. The color of eyes symbolizes the human. The fact that the "son looked exactly like the father" means that the father has also forgotten his color. Work—or "an important thing" as Mrs. Zilke says—is inhuman if it becomes all-important. The father joins the other men of strong true purpose who forget specific, small things which could destroy their narcissistic urge. There is also the wedding ring. The son is discovered chewing it by Mrs. Zilke and his father. The son calls it a "golden toy," meaning that he wants something to play with, to cling to in a hostile environment. But the father knows that he cannot permit the son to play with it: the ring is important for him because it *proves* his marriage to humanity. When both battle for possession, it falls on the carpet. Purdy shows us that the wedding is broken.

The "exquisite pain" felt by the father after his son kicks him in the groin is also felt by Lafe and Peaches in "Man and Wife." Both of them are filled with self-pity to such an extent that they cannot imagine life without it. Constantly complaining, they can be hurt by others whom they irritate. The strong true purpose becomes inverted. But the "lovely" narcissism remains the same. Lafe, like the father in the preceding story, has "no character." He has given up his color, his humanity, to one idea which he hates and loves: he believes he is homosexual. Lafe, however, does not realize that he seeks pity from Peaches and nothing else. She is merely a part of the image he has of himself. Peaches, on the other hand, is so self-centered that although she tries to play her role and offer pity, she can only pity herself: "I feel if it's what I am fearing I'd split open like a stone." Peaches then does not fit into his picture. Purdy's irony is corrosive and sad: two narcissists are married not to each other but to their complaints. There is one important symbol in "Man and Wife." The refrigerator is broken. This machine contains within it the mechanized existence of Lafe and Peaches Maud. It is variously described as "menacing," "clattering," "vacant," and each of these adjectives applies to their marriage. Furthermore, they speak to or think of the "crazy" refrigerator so much that it "grows in size" until it dominates their dull lives.

The harsh comedy in *Malcolm* arises from the compulsive need of narcissists to shape youthful Malcolm into an image of themselves. But he refuses to conform: he always has the stupidity or wisdom to repel their will to power over him. He is never their slave. The very first page of the novel introduces the pattern. Malcolm, who looks "like a foreigner," *seems* to be "expecting somebody." Purdy, however, implies that the young man is as others desire him—up to a point. The foreign quality and the silence—"he seldom spoke to anybody"—relate him to John Singer, another "odd" blank.

Mr. Cox cannot allow him to remain "untouched"; he is said to feel "responsible" for the part of the city where the young man resides. This astrologer decides to disregard Malcolm's humanity for his own "career and thought—not to say existence." He must make him conform to his narcissistic urge: "Either Mr. Cox must change the direction of his morning walks, which would be, if not a defeat, a total revolution in his way of life, or *he* must recognize the youth on the bench." Mr. Cox sends Malcolm to various addresses, hoping that he will be educated. The people he meets are similar to Mr. Cox (although they dislike "authority") and they also find that the youth remains unknown; they don't understand his unbroken humanity. Estel Blanc, for example, dresses elegantly. He wears "a somewhat long puce jacket with real diamond buttons." His entire existence is as artificial as his clothing. Estel is an undertaker (symbolically related to death) who glamorizes his profession as *art*. Because he is a Negro, he has a quality of defensive pride. All in all, Estel is a complete narcissist who remains puzzled that his advances are repelled by Malcolm: " 'I am puzzled,' Malcolm heard the baritone voice of Estel Blanc saying, 'by your coolness, detachment, and lack of receptivity.' "

The ability of Purdy to present the crazy comedy of narcissism is at its best in his portrayal of Madame Girard. Her monstrous self-love is based on power. She is married to Girard Girard, the tycoon, and she lives in The Chateau. She expects everyone around her to indulge her whims. However, like Peaches Maud she loves whining. Purdy describes her monstrosity by understatement or rather by exact description of what she thinks of the world—the comedy reflects her narcissistic *Weltanschauung*: "As Malcolm looked hastily about the great glass room beyond which one could catch glimpses of the ocean and the lights of cities—he caught sight of at least ten young men who were all seated on identical straight-back chairs—all facing Madame Girard, the sole member of her sex in the room—and all silent, like a mute chorus." These young men—and he is to be one of them—are her admirers; they are "identical" like the chairs because she has made them play things. Malcolm, unfortunately, does not acknowledge Madame Girard: he claims that she is drunk (as he called Mr. Cox a pederast). This only confirms her love for him. What a novelty, she thinks.

Malcolm eventually succumbs to the people around him (as does Singer), and he dies after marriage to Melba, the torch singer. Because he never gains "authority" to look at the world without rose-colored glasses, he has nothing to fall back upon. He has seen so much of deficient narcissism that he cannot embrace it; neither can he fully cope with it. Purdy tells us that Malcolm's death is as mysterious as his life: "Thus, the only proof that Malcolm had died and was buried, rested with Madame Girard herself, and in time her story became full of evasions." A blank ending!

Malcolm demonstrates that the comic and the horrifying are united. Both result from what William Van O'Connor has called the eruption of categories. Madame Girard and Mr. Cox refuse to see the world as it is. By jumping into the pool of Narcissus, they lose their character: they become mechanical. Now the mechanical can be laughed at (as Bergson suggested) because it is nonhuman; it can't be hurt; it can spring back. (The principle applies in cartoons.) Madame Girard and Mr. Cox and Estel Blanc are things which cannot die: she has the identical men; Mr. Cox has the stars; Estel has his diamond buttons. But the mechanical is ultimately horrifying. We think that these things cannot regain—do they want to?—their humanity. They have lost their *character* by self-love. And we, sensing our self-love, know that we can become their reflections. Thus we shudder.

New American Gothic deals, then, with self-love

that mechanizes people. Frankenstein becomes the archetype. I have tried to suggest that the concern with the one theme does not prevent highly individual treatment. Hazel Motes suffers from self-love; so does Mr. Cox. There is, however, a world of difference between them. It is dangerous to limit the achievement of new American Gothic by saying that it is repetitive or uninventive. The writers discussed show admirable creativity—something their heroes lack.

3   THE FAMILY

BECAUSE THE FAMILY IS usually considered a stable unit, new American Gothic tries to destroy it—the assumption is that if the family cannot offer security, nothing can. Narcissism causes the destruction. The parent usually loves himself more than his child; the child hates the power of the parent at the same time he wants it for himself. Rarely do we find "togetherness." Often new American Gothic uses a symbolic family. The reason is clear: the "real" family is so confusing, so shattered, that the parent or child flees from it. He searches for surrogate-figures, but the narcissistic circle asserts itself, and the same kind of needless destruction follows. Again it is necessary to stress the "flatness" of new American Gothic. Family *types* recur: there are the ineffectual child, the evil parent, occasionally the good parent. John W. Aldridge has called Capote's world "child-like." [1] The adjective can be applied to the image of the family in new American Gothic. Parent and child are frequently stunted by their dependence (willing or unwilling) on self-love; they never grow up.

Perhaps the best introduction to the family is *Other Voices, Other Rooms*. Here we see the Gothic flatness, the surrogate-figures, the concern with narcissism. Joel Harrison Knox is, as Mr. Aldridge tells us, searching for a father.[2] Never having "laid eyes" on Mr. Sansom (his mother has remarried), he has not really learned about society. He is locked in his private world and he wants—but is afraid—to escape. He has a "tired, imploring expression." Joel is at a crucial stage when we meet him: he can either turn inward completely—to "melt in a constant dream"—or learn to love others. He is Janus-faced.

In the first chapter Capote introduces two "fathers" who prepare the way for Mr. Sansom. Both Sam Radcliff and Jesus Fever give him a "lift" (introduce him to the new world). They are as ineffectual as his blood father. Radcliff says: "Remember, your Pa's your pa no matter what." The advice isn't very helpful because Joel does not know his father. Jesus Fever may have a "touch of the wizard in his yellow, spotted eyes," but he is "feeble" and "dreamy." After the boy arrives at Skulley's Landing, he discovers that his father is also feeble—in fact, he is at the point of death. That he throws red tennis balls down the steps (or, rather, drops them) indicates his child-like passivity. Joel finds that Mr. Sansom is as weak as he.

The turning into self is complete when he adopts Randolph. By loving him, he manages to love himself. Mr. Aldridge has demonstrated that Randolph is as "unreal as the fantastic creations of Joel's dream-world." [3] Randolph is loved because he is more of a projection of the boy's passive prettiness than an individual. Joel retreats into his own "girlish tenderness." Because he has been close to his aunt (in spite of their quarrels), failed to assert an active role with Idabel, and identified with Zoo, Joel loses his Janus-face: he turns towards Randolph as the beautiful-lady side of himself: "She beckoned to him, shining and silver, and he knew he must go; unafraid, not hesitating, he paused only at the garden's edge where, as though he'd forgotten something, he stopped and looked back at the bloomless descending blue, at the boy he had left behind."

In "Master Misery" Sylvia, like Joel, has left her family behind. The only unit she is part of in New York is that of Estelle and Henry but, as she says, "they were so excruciatingly married." They seem to have no room for her. Sylvia wants to stand apart from the family structure; however, she fears isolation. Capote shows us that the neurotic heroine adopts a monstrous, substitute family—Miss Mozart, Mr. Revercomb, even the Negro butler become her "parents." The interesting thing in the story is that again we discover a one-sided, melodramatic characterization of the parents. Mr. Revercomb is the "evil" father— evil like Cousin Randolph. He uses Sylvia; he plays with her soul. The warmth she finds in him (at least in her dreams) is incestuous; it parallels the closeness of Joel and his cousin-father. But the warmth vanishes as she finds him "sharp" and "cold"—a sadistic clinician. The weak, good father (seen as Mr. Sansom, Jesus Fever and Sam Radcliff) assumes the form of Oreilly. He is the conscience of Sylvia, her teacher. Although he teaches her that Mr. Revercomb is Master Misery, the "fellow who lives in the hollows of trees . . . and lurks in graveyards," he cannot really help her because of his own limitations. The good father flees by drinking. (Remember that Jesus Fever and Mr. Sansom die; Sam Radcliff leaves Joel.) He becomes an alcoholic clown, as child-like as Sylvia. At the end of the story Oreilly "travels in the blue," leaving his child in the "white sea."

In "Shut a Final Door" Walter is another neurotic adult. As Anna reminds him: "it's very compulsive, your malice, and you aren't too much to blame." He is a mean boy, always attacking others; he cannot keep his friends. When he flees from the city to the "stifling hotel," he thinks that he can find shelter. The room means so much to him that he is afraid, like a child, to leave it—"for what if he got lost?" But an evil parent enters.

The parent speaks over the phone. The "voice, dry and sexless and altogether unlike any he'd ever heard before," says: "Walter. You've known me a long time." The parent is like Mr. Revercomb—he threatens the existence of a weak child. Capote makes it quite clear that the parent-child relationship is crucial. After Walter's first call, he has a dream: he "hails" a procession of "black, funeral-like" cars and his father holds open the door of the first car. When Walter rushes to it, the "door slams shut, mashing off his fingers." Other people in the cars throw roses and Walter falls upon the roses—"pale blood" bleeds over the flowers. The dream tells us that Walter *sees* himself as a child hurt by an evil father who "kills with kindness." After he arrives at another hotel in Saratoga, he tries to find a good parent; he encounters a crippled woman who, he thinks, can take care of him. When the phone rings again, Walter clutches her to him as he cries: "Hold me, please." And the incident ends with: " 'Poor little boy,' she said, patting his back. 'My poor little boy: we're awfully alone in this world, aren't we?' And presently he went to sleep in her arms." Walter cannot keep the peace he finds at the side of the warm mother. He keeps running, and the voice catches up to him.

There is irony in "Miriam." Here the roles are reversed even more. Not only do we have an adult who is a child—we have a child who is an adult, the evil parent. First note that Mrs. H. T. Miller, although sixty-one, is as "oblivious as a mole burrowing a blind path." She says after buying Miriam the ticket: "I do hope I haven't done anything wrong." She is a complete innocent. Miriam, the girl, lacks any childlike quality whatsoever. She has authority; she offers advice: " 'But isn't that funny?' 'Moderately,' said Miriam, and rolled the peppermint on her tongue. Mrs. Miller flushed and shifted uncomfortably." The shifting continues: Miriam becomes as evil as Mr. Revercomb and Randolph when she plays with Mrs. Miller's soul. She refuses to leave, unless the woman says "please." She says another time: *Give it to me.*" Although Mrs. Miller turns to the good landlord, he cannot help because Miriam exists only in the woman's mind. The girl remains to say "Hello," not "Goodbye."

In "A Tree of Night" Capote returns to the usual psychological pattern. Kay is separated from her family; returning to college after the funeral of her uncle, she finds herself in a train with an odd couple who, after some polite talk (the man is a mute; only the woman says "honey"), take on the role of menacing parents. The woman tells Kay to drink, not to lie about having to leave them; the man strokes her cheek. These parents are interested in corrupting and punishing their child—at least she thinks so. Gradually Kay succumbs to their commands and loses her identity. The woman pulls the girl's "raincoat like a shroud above her head."

In the stories I have discussed, the child sinks at the end. Kay falls asleep; Sylvia says "I do not know what I want" while she walks in the sea; Joel moves in a trance; and Walter pushes "his face into the pillow." The evil parent destroys identity; the child returns to the womb.

Carson McCullers also deals with family tensions which result from the failure of any love but self-love. In *The Heart Is a Lonely Hunter*, for example, almost every family tie is broken. Mick's parents are not de-

scribed at great length, but the little we see of them
indicates that they neglect her many problems. The
first time we meet "Mama," we hear her say to Mick:
"What's the matter with you? What have you been
into now?" Mother then tells her to eat in the kitchen
because a roomer has brought his two sisters to dinner
—there isn't any space left for her. Dad is said to have
one thing on his mind—"ways he could have made
money and didn't." Both parents are shadows. They
only become full-bodied when the accident involving
Bubber occurs.

Although Mick knows that her parents mean well,
she recognizes that there is a gulf between them that
cannot be bridged. Mrs. McCullers presents a heart-
rending scene when Mick and Dad speak. The girl
senses that her father is awkward, old, and lonesome:
"And in his lonesomeness he wanted to be close to one
of his kids. . . . He felt like he wasn't much real use
to anybody." She stays with him a "good while," yet
can't tell him "about things in her mind." Mick desperately searches for surrogate-parents, and she finds
one in John Singer. That he is inscrutable (her parents
are not, unfortunately) appeals to her. But the relationship is distorted. He, like Dad and Mama, doesn't understand her. Mrs. McCullers' family relationships are
more pathetic than Capote's. She presents parents who
are so passive that they cannot control their destinies
—let alone those of their children. Dad is as weak as
Mr. Sansom, but he is more than a pair of yellow eyes.
In other words, the parents are given substance. Even
when Mrs. McCullers presents an evil parent, she
views the evil as all too human.

Doctor Copeland, a strong man, is, however, like
Dad in not getting along well with his children. His
true purpose is always before his eyes, and his children
become mere adjuncts to it. When Portia says to him

that they should "quit this here quarreling," the doctor cannot understand her. Later when Willie and High-boy enter, he tries to tell them that "I put all of my trust and hope in you. And all I get is blank misunderstanding and idleness and indifference." He does not see that they want to live their own "worthless" lives because, at least partially, they are fighting his evil strength. Doctor Copeland, indeed, regards the whole Negro race as children. He teaches the children he delivers in the same way he teaches his own: "they must thrust from their shoulders—the yoke of submission and slothfulness." Ironically, the rebellion he teaches is turned against him—all of his children refuse to obey the mission.

The pathos of Copeland's plight reaches a climax at the end. Ill, depressed, no longer strong, he returns to the country house of his father-in-law. The prodigal son has forgotten his mission. His good father tells him: "Yes, I glad to have you. I believe in all kinfolks sticking together—blood kin and marriage kin. I believe in all us struggling along and helping each other out, and some day us will have a reward in the Beyond."

The muted incest that is evident in Capote's families (and in Mick and Dad) asserts itself. Biff is not happily married to Alice because, as he admits, he likes cripples and he is bisexual. Actually his problem is impotence. After Alice dies, he cannot forget her. He tries to find a family tie. Singer comes into focus and then blurs because he is too "uncanny." The other person is Mick. Biff, attracted to Mick, has no real sexual desire for her (or for anyone) but he has to have a "child" so that he can feel more powerful. At one point he thinks: "To adopt a couple of little children. A boy and a girl. About three or four years old so that they will always feel like he was their own father. Their Dad. Our

Father. The little girl like Mick (or Baby?) at that age." Biff's dream cannot come true. He can never admit to Mick that he wants her; little does he know that she is searching for an understanding parent. In this "family romance" Mrs. McCullers deals with the reversal of roles. Copeland is strong father and weak child; Mick is separated from Dad and Mama but, at the end, she is a breadwinner; Biff is more of a mother than a father. The crosscurrents flow together in Singer's case. The mute becomes the family tie each person is looking for. However, he is false. The stable father-confessor (or oppressed child) shoots himself.

In *Reflections in a Golden Eye* there are no family ties. Mrs. McCullers seems to imply that these monstrous characters cannot even beget children to hurt. Alison's situation is relevant: after her baby is born, she and her husband, Major Langdon, discover that the baby's index and third fingers are grown together. The Major wishes for the baby's death—later he feels "nothing except relief" when she does die. Despite the fact that there are no children in the novelette, Mrs. McCullers does suggest unbalanced "community." Major Langdon is so completely dependent on the Pendertons, especially Leonora, that he is regarded as a "third member" of the family. His role as husband to Alison is usurped by Anacletto, the houseboy. Leonora Penderton enjoys Langdon as a lover because she merely regards her own husband as an unruly "son." The interlocking of the two couples (with the addition of Private Williams and Anacletto) creates an odd family tragedy—the suffocation in the book is partly explained by the childish dependence of each character upon another. Perhaps the image of Williams secretly eating a candy bar suggests the tone of all the relationships.

There is no doubt about the family situation in *The*

Member of the Wedding. Frankie Addams, like Mick, discovers that her Papa doesn't really know her. He plays a minor role in her life. She wonders when he is "coming home from town." It is interesting to note that Papa, according to her, has a *"we"* in the store, not in her. Papa is so "set in his ways" that "he [does] not listen to things she said or new suggestions." He seems to nod throughout the novel. And when he does not nod, he impatiently asks, Is the toast burning? Where have you been?

Because Frankie is not the we of her father, she attaches herself to the wedding of her brother. She is searching for new parents. She wants the devoted care she has never received from her widower father. Therefore she glamorizes the new family: "We will belong to so many clubs that we can't even keep track of them. We will be members of the whole world." Frankie is shocked, of course, when she learns that her new parents do not want her—they have their own lives and future children to consider. Actually the wedding is not the only surrogate family she possesses (at least in her mind). Berenice and John Henry are the other family. But the Negro servant, although she tries to counsel her, is constantly aware of past love. As John B. Vickery writes: "Berenice is nevertheless committed to an adult view of Frankie's trials with the result that most of her advice cannot be absorbed into the imaginative world of the child; adult and child . . . are from different countries." [4] And John Henry, of course, cannot give support to Frankie. He is too childish (or too adult) to be able to teach her that she is a "freak." She refuses to listen to him. And he dies.

Thus *The Member of the Wedding,* unlike most of Capote's fiction, does not present the misery-giving parent. Frankie's parents—her Papa, Berenice, even Jarvis—are not daemonic intruders; on the contrary, they are good adults who somehow cannot communicate with her. The pathetic isolation of each in his own world has no real cause or cure. Parenthood is horrifyingly weak—it cannot destroy or create. Mr. Vickery's words about the "total vision of love" can apply equally well to the family: "It is fragmented and disconnected, contributed to by each of the characters and each of the stories, and grasped in greater or lesser degree by a very few of them." [5]

Unlike Capote and Mrs. McCullers, Salinger presents the family in all of its complexity. In the early stories we find the same passivity or hostility of the parents along with an idealized view which, in the later stories, dominates everyone. The family, in fact, serves as an index of decline from Gothic to mysticism. "The Stranger," a typical early story of Salinger, appeared in the December 1, 1945 issue of *Collier's*. The plot is simple: Babe Gladwaller, a recently discharged veteran, finds it difficult to speak about war to Mrs. Polk, the former fiancee of his buddy. He wants to tell her that soldiers don't light cigarettes before shells explode in their faces, that his buddy died in an unheroic way. The inner tension is great. Babe resists, however, by rationalizing that a woman cannot understand such matters. He leaves Mrs. Polk's apartment with his kid sister, Mattie, who has patiently awaited their departure. He finds some pleasure in watching her skip and jump.

"The Stranger" offers a clue to the role of the family. Salinger suggests that wounded adults (like Babe and later Seymour Glass) cannot wed the world—their anxiety interferes with their parenthood. But at the same time, they worship children so much that the children become rulers of their spirit. The horrifying reversal of roles in "Miriam"—the adult as child, the child as adult—is here sympathetically presented, but the reversal is still out of hand. We don't usually meet children in war stories, but if we take Mattie as a symbol of "wise innocence," we can understand why Salinger makes her the "ally" of Babe. The veteran's only attachment to social living is through his imaginative response to her happy movements.

The lack of communication between man and woman, the almost incestuous closeness of "father" (or brother) and daughter (or sister), appear in many other Salinger stories. In "A Perfect Day for Bananafish" Seymour is isolated from his wife and mother-in-law. While Muriel and her mother converse about his illness, never confronting it in any way, he is on the beach with Sybil (note the name). He enjoys the company of this wise child more than nonsensical adults. He swims with her—a symbol, perhaps, of his desire to return to the womb. (And his tale of the bananafish is, on one level, an anxiety-dream of a mature relationship with a woman.) That Sybil is safe, inscrutable, happy is made even more evident after Seymour returns to the confines of the hotel. There he is disturbed by a woman with "zinc salve" on her nose who, he thinks, looks surreptitiously at his feet. The incident is a prelude to his retreat into suicide, while Muriel is asleep in the room which smells of nail-lacquer remover.

Although the two stories present the lack of family love caused by narcissism or plain misunderstanding, they don't employ the wedding as complete symbol as does "For Esmé—With Love and Squalor." The structure of this war story is complex. The narrator, after receiving a wedding invitation, describes his past adventures during World War II. Then, he tells us, he was depressed as a soldier until he met Esmé. She is a more mature Sybil—that is, she realizes some of the horrors of adult life. Esmé has lived in London during

the blitz, but she has survived through repeated acts of
kindness and love. Her survival is symbolized by two
facts: she sings in a choir and she wears her dead
father's watch. Esmé understands that the narrator
can have a breakdown. She volunteers to write letters
to him, hoping that she can save his incomplete self
from destruction. The next section of the story is, as
the narrator tells us, "squalid and moving." He sees
himself as X. Close to the point of breakdown, X discovers love through Esmé. She sends him the watch,
and this gift has such magical power that it produces
rewarding sleep; it helps X to keep his faculties intact.

The relation of Esmé and the narrator is ideal and
"incestuous." It is not part of the everyday world, the
real wedding. We remember the opening lines in which
the narrator describes his present marriage. From all
indications his wife and mother-in-law are like Muriel
and her mother. They do not want him to be a member
of Esmé's wedding in England. They treat him as a
sick child. This treatment so disturbs his faculties
that he must recapture Esmé and the love she represented through retrospection. Thus the genesis of the
story.

The anxiety of the war veterans, their separation
from the "real" family, their desperate adoption of
ideal sisters or daughters—all these are in *The Catcher
in the Rye*. Salinger realizes that the attempt for self-
definition is especially confused during adolescence.
The self must become whole in the face of the crowd;
it must battle against libidinal drives. The inability to
reconcile itself to the super-ego and id, to become a
unit, can lead the half-formed self to turn more inward
until it is isolated from everything else. *The Catcher
in the Rye* is "universal" because Holden's schizoid
condition is so normal in our society. He dislikes
"phonies" such as Hollywood actors, the headmaster

of Pencey Prep, Ernie, when he plays piano for the public, and "old Luce," an expert on sex. These people have submitted, he thinks, to the demands of the public. Holden believes that he wants to develop himself in a narcissistic environment. He is determined to flee from the phonies, hoping that he can find what he is looking for (which he, himself, does not understand) in kinds of experience alien to materialistic society.

This reason compels him to remember his dead brother, Allie, even after he writes the composition about the mitt. His vision of Allie's funeral is horrifying because he sees the reactions of his relatives who are interested in the flower arrangements rather than the dead boy. Holden also remembers the Eskimo in The Museum of Natural History who, like his brother, has achieved peace, "staying right where he was." Eternal "childhood" is one means of escape; silence is another. (Note the reappearance of the nonreflecting, peaceful mute.) But Holden also realizes that such visions of complete withdrawal are impossible for the moment.

Holden's relation to Allie (and later Phoebe) is similar to that of the other Salinger heroes. He likes brothers and sisters more than parents. He feels uncomfortable with Mr. Spencer, his teacher at Pency Prep, noticing the ugly habits of the old man. Certainly he cannot accept his theory that "Life *is* a game. Holden admits characteristically to "Old Spencer" that he has not communicated with his parents. Presumably, he knows that full of self-love, they don't really care about him. They are *absent* when he does return home.

Holden believes that he has one strong, good parent in Mr. Antolini, his old teacher. After Mr. Antolini offers some advice—"The mark of the immature man is that he wants to die nobly for a cause, while the mark of the mature man is that he wants to live humbly for one"—and coffee, Holden goes to sleep. Then he wakes suddenly to find his father's hand on his head. Parental love is viewed as unnatural, "scary." Is Mr. Antolini evil? The question disturbs Holden so much that he renounces him and flees back to children.

He communicates with Phoebe, his kid sister, who knows him better than do his parents. He even goes to Central Park with her. At one point Holden thinks that he would like to be a catcher in the rye. He sees himself as a perfect parent (one he has not known), a hero, who can save children from falling off the "crazy cliff" into the adult world. He will save them from understanding the torment of social living; indeed, he will try to make them stay right where they are, unworried about self-definition. Holden has the dream for a moment because he is a practical person. He views childhood more realistically when he watches Phoebe on the carrousel. Salinger makes it clear that Holden sees Phoebe as being more adjusted to grabbing for the gold ring (symbolic of Ideals?) than he is. She is unaware that the "real" world is harsh, that a haze clouds her eyes, and that she has to achieve self-definition. As an experienced outsider, Holden knows that although he cannot participate in the symbolic ride of childhood, it is nevertheless more beautiful and instructive than narcissistic parenthood.

I have suggested that in his later stories Salinger's gospel of love embraces the family. Teddy may have quarrels with his self-centered parents but he understands them. The wise child—now a genius!—loves all. Seymour Glass makes the heroic gesture of accepting Muriel and her family; he calls them noble, brave, good. Zooey loves his mother almost as much as he does Seymour, his brother. The impressive portrayal of estrangement between parent and child and the ideal, almost incestuous union of wise children become one huge embrace. This is why I cannot agree with Paul Levine, who writes:

> In a vast world full of misunderstanding and estrangement, the sensitive innocent must turn in towards the family to find the ultimate love and communication that is so lacking in the outside world. It is through the family that he retains his equilibrium, balancing his moral integrity against the social pressures of the outside world. Thus the family becomes the place where self and society meet, where the moral and ethical realms are reconciled.[6]

The "intimate love and communication" is falsely gained. Salinger has reached the point where the catcher in the rye lives with the Glasses.

Flannery O'Connor's concern with family relationships and the terror they inspire is as strong as that of Salinger. But she pulls no punches. In *Wise Blood* (as well as *The Violent Bear It Away*) she parallels Christian and un-Christian families. Although Hazel Motes' mother believes strongly in Jesus, she does not see that her lack of maternal love is responsible for her son's rebellious nature—not carrying over her love for Jesus, she punishes unruly Hazel: "Jesus died to redeem you," she reminds him. To which he answers: "I never ast him." Later he continues to rebel by sleeping with Mrs. Leora Watts, a mother-surrogate, and by proclaiming the Church Without Christ.

Hazel's estrangement from his mother is similar to Sabbath Lily Hawks' estrangement from her father. The woman who poses as a child has a "short sharp nose," and the sharpness also applies to her will. She and her father, a false preacher, hate each other so much that they live in continual hostility. They both want to escape from their commitments. Sabbath Lily decides to rebel (her father no longer needs her) by seducing Hazel who, at the same time, wants to sleep with her. The narcissistic children set up housekeeping. They need a child of their own. Enoch helps by stealing the mummy from the museum, wrapping it up, and leaving it on their doorstep. Opening the bundle, Sabbath Lily has an "empty" look but after being "out" a few minutes, she cuddles the mummy and sings to it. Now the union is complete. We have an "unholy family." [7]

The same kind of monstrous family is evident in Miss O'Connor's stories. Usually the parent imposes his strength in a fierce, Old-Testament way; we are back to Walter's phone voice. In "A Good Man Is Hard to Find" the Grandmother's self-centeredness inhibits her son, Bailey, to such an extent that he obeys all of her whims. Later she gives the same well-meaning advice, the same false love, to the Misfit: "She saw the man's face twisted close to her as if he were going to cry and she murmured, 'Why you're one of my babies. You're one of my own children.' " The Misfit responds by shooting her "three times through the chest."

Unlike the Grandmother, the parents in "The River" are "skeletons" who don't even have the strength to take care of their son. Mama is "ill"; Dad says "for Christ's sake fix him." The parents discharge him to the baby sitter. (Note how they are comparatively absent—like Holden's parents.) Mrs. Cronnin, the baby sitter, is the familiar parent in Miss O'Connor's fiction. Like Mrs. Motes and the Grandmother, she is a "firm believer" who by carrying love for Jesus over to her son, hurts him. She forcefully takes him to a baptism ceremony. The irony lies in the fact that although the child fears the baptism, after a while he sees in the preacher and Mrs. Cronnin new parents who *care*. He returns to his apartment and confronts his parents (they, he senses, don't want him back). He knows that however they may act toward him, he *counts*. In the early morning he knows "what he wanted to do." Returning to the river, he drowns himself.

"The Artificial Nigger" views the family relationships I have discussed in greater depth. The strong father is Mr. Head, who regards himself as a "suitable guide for the young." But he, like the room in which he wakes, is "full of moonlight." He suffers from a narcissistic delusion. Thinking "age was a choice blessing," he undertakes a "moral mission": to teach his grandson, Nelson, the way to live. Miss O'Connor uses classical images to establish the irony of the situation: Mr. Head "might have been Vergil summoned in the middle of the night to go to Dante, or better, Raphael, awakened by a blast of God's light to fly to the side of Tobias." The very use of these images serves to make the story mythic and Mr. Head foolish. Mr. Head decides to take Nelson on a tour of the city underworld. He will teach him to be "content to stay at home for the rest of his life." Nelson is too smart for his own good, his grandfather thinks (not realizing the irony), and the trip will have a beneficial effect: it will convert Nelson and establish his own greatness.

After they get on the train, they notice their reflections: "There he saw a pale ghost-like face scowling at him beneath the brim of a pale ghost-like hat. His grandfather looking quickly too, saw a different ghost, pale but grinning, under a black hat." Mr. Head and Nelson are both ghosts because they have not discovered their limitations. They don't see their sinfilled bodies. Nelson is startled to find during the trainride that he is afraid. He abandons his smart-aleck comments and he "weds" his grandfather. He is glad

16779

that he does. His admiration for Mr. Head's wisdom knows no bounds when the old man gives him secret information about the city's sewer system. But Miss O'Connor shows us that the ideal father-son relationship disintegrates. In the city Mr. Head loses his way. He is no longer the perfect guide. He becomes the familiar shadow of a parent we have met before. Nelson's overwhelming fear returns: he begins to see that he must assume command. He must become the wise child. The transformation is incomplete. Nelson continues to blunder, trying to find the way back to the train station. Suddenly he runs into an old woman who shouts to Mr. Head: "Your boy has broken my ankle!". . . "Police!" The grandfather declares, "This is not my boy," when the policeman arrives, "I never saw him before." Nelson knows now what the boy in "The River" and Frankie Addams do: no parent can ever abandon his narcissism: "Nelson's fingers fall out of [Mr. Head's] flesh."

It is at this point in "The Artificial Nigger" that the Gothic family disappears. We find the solemn conversion of Mr. Head. When he begins "to feel the depth of his denial," he "[knows] now what time would be like without light and man would be like without salvation." Nelson finds that although he sees his grandfather's limitations, he sympathizes with his plight. Both share the "amazing" vision of the artificial nigger: they see the statue as some "monument to another's victory that brought them together in their common defeat." The fact that a Negro can have a statue dedicated to him, they think, shows what a mysterious world it is! After their differences are dissolved "like an action of mercy," they board the train. Nelson and Mr. Head admit that in the future they will stay at home. Humility comes into focus as it does in the Glass family.

In "The Life You Save May Be Your Own" we return to the domineering parent. The old woman does not "[change] her position"; she stands with "one hand *fisted* on her hip" (my italics). She treats her deaf daughter, Lucynell, as a silly child. And she wants her to marry someone who will assume responsibility for her. Mr. Shiftlet, who comes to the farm, seems a likely candidate to the old woman. "Ravenous for a son-in-law," she slowly guides him to Lucynell: the girl won't be any great trouble; she can't complain much. In fact, she manages to sell Lucynell to Mr. Shiftlet. The horror of selling blood relations is even more shocking than the other actions I have mentioned. This horror is intensified when Mr. Shiftlet, taking a hint from his mother-in-law, abandons Lucynell. Completely evil (like the Misfit), he nevertheless realizes that selling and abandoning people are disgusting: it takes the following comment of a boy to strengthen the insight: "You go to the devil! . . . My old woman is a flea bag and yours is a stinking pole cat!"

As expected, Miss O'Connor's new novel, *The Violent Bear It Away*, contains the evil parent and the innocent child, but the striking thing is that the Gothic family is magnified: the family ties are so close that one critic has viewed the novel as "an elaborate fantasy of what one can only call homosexual incest." [8] If we regard the incest as that of will rather than sex, we are close to the truth not only of this novel but of the other Gothic fictions.

To begin with the rigid parent. The great-uncle is a self-appointed preacher who, like Mr. Head and Mrs. Motes, undertakes the religious instruction of the orphan boy, Tarwater. He thinks that he has learned by fire; anxious to perpetuate his "seed," he teaches him "in the evils that befall prophets; in those that come from the world, which are trifling, and those that come from the Lord and burn the prophet clean." The great-uncle wants Tarwater to mirror him. The boy, as "precocious" or "innocent" as Malcolm, cannot accept his great-uncle as father. Every time he preaches to him, he rebels verbally. But he is so influenced by the great-uncle that he is slowly adopting a crazy narcissism which assumes it is the Truth. Like him he is self-centered. The inner tensions of Tarwater are given body. They are projected as a "stranger" who talks to him. At first the stranger is viewed as a "wise voice," a "mentor," someone who *knows*. The stranger instructs him to abandon the "life the old man had prepared for him." Be yourself! he whispers. But the boy isn't sure whether he should be himself or his great-uncle. The stranger becomes sinister.

The ambivalence towards his father-image (both the dead great-uncle and the stranger) is intensified by a third father, Rayber. Rayber, Tarwater's uncle, is an atheist who, like the old man, has a mission: he wants to teach the boy the new faith of atheism. If he can convert him, turn him from the false prophecy of the old man, then he will exult in his power. He will love himself even more. Tarwater's ambivalence is paralleled in Rayber. Rayber also has been influenced by the old man who kidnapped and baptized him at the age of seven. He has never come to terms with the father-image. He sees his own problems in the orphan, his "own imprisoned image." By winning Tarwater away from the old man, he will save *himself*.

Gradually the novel focuses on Bishop, the idiot son of Rayber. Tarwater has been instructed to baptize him, to save him from his atheistic father. If he does this, the orphan knows he has submitted to the great-uncle. Rayber has a "horrifying love" for the idiot son. He loves him so much that he would like to kill his unthinking person. Rayber and Tarwater converge on Bishop and kill him. As Rayber looks out the window at the lake where Tarwater has baptized and drowned the idiot, he "stood there waiting for the raging pain, the intolerable hurt that was due to begin, so that he could ignore it, but he continued to feel nothing." Bishop is destroyed by "dull, mechanical" narcissism.

To sum up: the great-uncle, the stranger, the uncle are evil parents who thrust their narcissistic designs upon innocent children. But ironies abound: the innocent Tarwater becomes so imbued with the plan (as he fights it) that he becomes an evil parent for Bishop. Rayber thinks he is an innocent child-victim, not an evil parent. In other words, the roles are distorted, inverted; they merge into a monstrous family in which parents and children do not know their identities.

The extreme family ties are so crucial in *The Violent Bear It Away* that Algene Baliff has seen the novel as a kind of allegory of "primitive Protestant experience":

> One of the distinguishing features of Protestantism has been its belief in direct, private, and intimate connection with God. . . . At the same time, however, Protestantism has always been identified with, if not actually held responsible for, the new social organizations which have issued in what we call "modern man"—man alienated from himself and others. Furthermore, Protestantism has long been associated with modern man's attempt to be "self-made," to create himself, to become, so to speak, his own father—an aspiration that suggests limitless possibilities for getting itself mixed up somewhere along the dark psychic line with the kind of homosexual, incestuous fantasy that Miss O'Connor insinuates into her novel.[9]

With this comment in mind, we can see how Flannery O'Connor may have a Catholic family in the background—Jesus and Mary and Joseph—a family in which the father-son relationship is tempered by the mother. Unlike the Protestant family, the Catholic family is well-rounded; roles are carefully defined; identity is considerably less ambiguous. Although this kind of "religious" view of the family illuminates Miss O'Connor's fiction, it does not really help to explain the same family types in the fiction of Capote, Mrs. McCullers, and Salinger—save by indirection. New American Gothic may be religious: it may show us Protestant failings; but it is safer to regard the family types as similar because of narcissism, not Protestantism. Other critics may equate the two.

For example, it is difficult to give a religious cause for the family in John Hawkes' fiction. He seems simply to regard adults as perpetual children, seeking strong parents. Such is the case in *Charivari*, his earliest published work. Here Henry Van, about to be married, is a lost child. He dreams characteristically that he is a "drowning baby." Although he manages to convey a "solid frontier" to others, he is constantly "perturbed" because he does not want to enter adult life. The wedding—remember Seymour Glass'—represents a terrible finality to childish dependence. On the big day Henry flees, but his father comes for him: "The parson sat waiting, stiffbacked and with a scowl on his face. He held his hat in his lap.

'Hello Father, what a pleasant surprise.'

'I've come to take you back, Henry.'

'Yes, sir.' There was nothing left to do." Like Tarwater and Rayber, Henry talks to a projection of the anxiety-provoking parent. The "Expositor," as he is called, constantly threatens: "You'll catch your death of cold when you walk in the snow." Henry excuses himself: "I was too old." Later he finds that the child he has expected to be born right after the marriage (otherwise, why marry Emily?) is not coming. For a while he can remain safe, dependent in middle-age.

Family relationships bind the various insane incidents in *The Cannibal*. Hawkes seems to imply that distorted, violent families parallel (or cause?) crazy love of the "fatherland." In "Part Two—1914" we meet the Snows. Ernst, the wounded son, is said to be "under his father's thumb." Family life is a constant battle. Unlike his mother who had never succumbed to Herr Snow's aggressive narcissism, he finds that he loses often. Ernst duels as a pastime, but even in a match his father enters "like a fat indignant judge, his face white with rage," and tells him and his friends that they are "fools." Herr Snow is so domineering that he also directs his son's love life. He instructs him how to court Stella: "A little aggression is needed."

What happens to such a son? Because Ernst has been unable to resist his terrifying father, not even to show as much strength as his mother, he tries to capture ideals: love, Stella, the fatherland. He becomes a fanatic. We have the same pattern of *The Violent Bear It Away*: afraid of the parent's narcissistic strength, the child adopts his own mission (he too can be strong!) and by doing so, becomes a weak reflection of the parent. Unsure of love or strength, Ernst is a menace: the sudden appearance of his "dangerous, unpleasant face" is likened to world war.

Stella is such a fitting partner for Ernst because she is also maimed by the family. Like Carson McCullers' girls she thinks of her father "as one she did not know. He was so old he never understood." Her mother is also too sick and child-like to offer any advice. Mother "lay in bed day after day, the spring, summer years dragging by, with only her head two hands long above the sheets, her eyes fastened together, motionless until some forgotten whim, surge of strength, drove her from the bed." Stella becomes compulsive:

she is sadistic because she wants to lash back at her parents, to be *strong*. For her as well as Ernst, love is contemplated as strength or weakness. When they marry, "she, not he, was the soldier, luring him on against the fence, under the thicket, forcing him down the back road through the evening." Stella is his master. She enjoys taking care of him after he is wounded in battle and becomes "as bothersome and old as all unhealthy people." The irony is that Ernst looks "just like Father" to her.

The final meeting of Ernst and his father is striking. Herr Snow pursues Gerta the servant and as he is ready to catch her, they enter the room in which the wounded son is resting. Instinctively the father says: "He's not sick!" And the son dies, "with his mouth twisted with dislike." To which we have the bitter reply: "he's only feigning."

The terror of the family is handed down. The son of Stella and Ernst is also wounded: when he returns from the second war, "with his stump and steel canes, with special steel loops circling up about his wrists for extra support, he had not added even one bare number to the scratched-out roster of the drunken Census-Taker." He marries and lives with his wife in an old movie house. They have no children.

The conflict between parents and children is elaborated in other ways. The Duke stalks and kills a boy for his supper. He is simply acting out in more insane ways the designs of Herr Snow. Jutta, Stella's sister, is the mother of the boy and a girl, Selvaggia. Selvaggia is a crucial character in the novel because, like all the other children, she is alone. Her mother is too interested in lovemaking with Zizendorf and the others to watch her. Stella, who should know better, resents "Selvaggia and her brother for bearing no resemblance to the family." Balamir, the lunatic who adopts Stella as a mother, thinks of himself as "an Emperor's son." He tries vainly to be the "image" of the Kaiser.

Appropriately enough, Hawkes ends *The Cannibal* with this scene:

> Selvaggia opened the door and crept into the room. She looked more thin than ever in the light of day, wild-eyed from watching the night and the birth of the Nation.
>
> "What's the matter, Mother? Has anything happened?"
>
> I [Zizendorf] answered instead of Jutta, without looking up, and my voice was vague and harsh; "Nothing. Draw those blinds and go back to sleep . . ."
>
> She did as she was told.

These few lines reveal the tone of the family: the innocent child wants to know meanings; the parents are wrapped in their own designs; the "birth of the Nation" is joined to the obedient "death" of Selvaggia.

In *The Goose on the Grave* Hawkes elaborates the portrayal of the innocent child in conflict with the adult world. When we first see Adeppi, he is watching his mother's corpse being carried off. "One of Italy's covey of fragile doves," he cannot live without any sheltering parent, and he turns from one adult to another, seeking the good one. Nino, a wounded soldier, becomes a father for Adeppi. But he is so mixed-up and wild that he only places the boy in more horrifying situations. He shows him lust and corruption; he toys with his soul. One incident is especially memorable. Nino decides to leave town and he runs to tell Adeppi to say farewell: "Nino ran straight to Adeppi. The soldier did not touch him, did not put a hand on his arm, but placed the muzzle against the boy's temple. The gun was steady." He does not shoot, but the "bewildered" expression of Adeppi is never to leave him after this initiation.

Searching for love, he finds other fathers. Edouard, an old playboy, adopts him because he likes boyish singing. But Jacopo, the accordion player, intrudes to strike out at Edouard and run away with the boy. These fathers, offering violent affection, are not more stable than he. In the midst of this "infernal" landscape Adeppi finds that one parent believes in the "holy family." Dolce, the priest, adopts him. Although he is also disturbed by guilt, he does believe in the parents Jacopo, Nino, and Edouard neglect—Jesus, Mary, and the saints. Thus Hawkes makes us remember the peace Adeppi enjoyed when he stopped running to stare at the madonna: "The madonna peered fiercely from this weight, suffering in the sunlight. Mysteriously burdened, she gazed with enamel face across the city and held up her empty arms. The thick skirt and wear of the weather hid nothing, the woodcarver had sculptured his madonna still with child, to look down on this square of small boys." Adeppi and Dolce know this: the good parent is immortal.

James Purdy does not supply a vision of the good parent. He simply gives us insight into the narcissism of parents who refuse to allow their children to grow up. We are back to daily horror, not transforming visions. I have already discussed "Color of Darkness." Here the father gives an immediate impression of weakness: he is afraid of himself and his son, Baxter. When Baxter gets close to him, he fears that he "might know everything." Anything which is out-of-the-ordinary disturbs his false order: toys, crying, swallowing a wedding ring. The father resembles the weak, self-centered parents of Stella and Frankie Addams: he grunts with "exquisite pain."

Again the family structure is so shattered that both father and son seek surrogate figures. Mrs. Zilke functions as substitute mother for them. The father always asks her advice; he wants her comfort: "You know, I am old." Mrs. Zilke constantly tells him not to worry. Baxter, of course, turns to her because his real mother is dead and his father is so narcissistically weak. Although the father realizes the real structure of the family, he cannot change: "He envied in a way Mrs. Zilke's command over everything. She understood, it seemed, everything she dealt with, and she remembered and could identify all the things which came into her view and under her jurisdiction." *He* cannot bring about a decisive difference. Purdy implies that the family structure changes somewhat—affection between father and son enters—when Baxter swallows the ring. Even then our last view of the father is: he "nodded from the floor where he twisted in his pain." Mrs. Zilke cannot help him to rise.

Ethel, the mother, in "Why Can't They Tell You Why?" is also a weakling. Like Salinger's Eloise she is always on the defensive; she wards off anxiety by talking compulsively—at least she thinks so. When we see her, she is talking on the phone to Edith Gainesworth. She complains that she is not being cared for: the government should give *her*, a widow, a pension. Paul, her son, is also weak and like the other ineffectual children we have met, he attempts to fight his parent. The only objects that can give him comfort and love and strength in this alien environment are the photographs of his dead father. Paul looks upon the father as an ideal—a grown-up Jimmy Jimmereeno—who can help him. The photographs are promises of life.

One evening Ethel discovers Paul asleep near his father's photographs. So incensed by the rebellion against her narcissistic order, she asks him why he loves his father. When Paul refuses to reply, she looks down at him as though "seeing him for the first time, noting with surprise how thin and puny he was, and how disgusting was one small mole that hung from his starved-looking throat." She lashes out at him for calling her "Mama" because she "could not see how this was her son." She continues to ask why, threatening to send him to the asylum, if he does not answer. Finally her nerves are so "bad" that she imagines a "mouse had gotten under her clothes." She forces Paul to throw the photographs into the furnace. He shrieks: "They're Daddy." And she chases him like an animal, trying to make him cough up the other photographs he has swallowed.

The weak, narcissistic parent, the crucified child, appear in *63: Dream Palace*. Parkhearst Cratty and Grainger are introduced in the strange prelude. Both are "dead" creatures, drunk and alone. Purdy immediately shows us their dream-like limitations. Parkhearst relates the story of Fenton Riddleway and his brother, Claire. In the park one evening Parkhearst, wandering aimlessly, meets Fenton, an "actually lost" adolescent. He decides to adopt the riddle, show him off to Grainger, the great woman. Purdy shows us the rather odd reversal of roles. Parkhearst is a child-like adult "who must not be crossed in the full possession of his freedom, one who must be left to follow his own whims and visions." And Grainger is so self-indulgent that she "draws her circle of people to her." She says "If everything . . . could be a garden with the ones you always want and with drinking forever and ever." These childish parents make Fenton their own.

What forces Fenton to call these parents "ideal"? Because he is alone with Claire in the big city—as alone as Paul or Baxter—he feels that he must find something. He cannot continue to go to all-night movies where strangers molest him. So when he meets his new parents he wears their clothes, he adopts their views. Fenton loses his humanity as he succumbs to

his *vita nuova*: "A new life was beginning for him."
He actually becomes a crazy reflection. But his brother
Claire is in the way. Claire does not want to leave the
house on 63rd Street for the dream palaces of self-love.
He wants to lie in bed, even with horrible bugs,
rather than adopt new ways of life. A pathetic creature
who loves and needs Fenton, he forces his older
brother into an awkward position. The only solution is
murder. Fenton strangles Claire. Although he "would
never feel such tenderness for any other person," he
must destroy him because he has simply become a
narcissistic reflection of his false parents. He buries
Claire in the attic, with a "gauzy kind of veil, like a
wedding veil." Fenton returns him to the dead, good
mother: "At the very end before he carried him upstairs and deposited him, he forced himself to kiss the
dead stained lips he had stopped, and said, "Up we go
then, motherf——"

We are back at the beginning. The narcissistic parent wins despite his weakness: he imposes his design
upon the ineffectual child, who begins to reflect him.
But the victory is hollow because destruction is always
present for both. Only at rare times does the dream of
past or future happiness, the love between parent and
child, the knowledge of correct rules, enter to give
peace. Because new American Gothic offers no solution to family strife, it produces that shudder at the
"edge of being," when the microcosm breaks down:
nothing is left; no one can help.

IN OLD GOTHIC we encounter the haunted castle, the voyage into the forest, and the reflection. Walpole, Monk Lewis, and Mrs. Radcliffe do not use these images in any psychologically acute way: they remain mere props. But the inheritors of old Gothic regard these images as "objective correlatives" of the psyche. Thus Hawthorne and Henry James—to name only two—view the castle as the outpost of authoritarianism; the voyage as the flight from such authoritarianism into new directions of strength or love; the reflection as the two-sidedness of motives, the "falseness" of human nature. The pattern exists in *The House of the Seven Gables* and "The Jolly Corner."

New American Gothic uses the same images. It is unnecessary here to prove that Capote and the others have read Walpole or Henry James—such proof cannot demonstrate how *they* use the images, nor can it explain the psychological accuracy or literary power of their images. In the following essay I assume that these crucial components of new American Gothic provide the scene (in Kenneth Burke's sense) for the distortions of narcissism and the wars in the family. Without them Gothic could not exist.

I have already mentioned that new American Gothic presents ambivalent characters who want to see the big world but are afraid to leave the little world. They are locked in narcissism; often they enjoy such imprisonment. I suggest that the "haunted castle" in new American Gothic usually functions as the metaphor of confining narcissism, the private world. There are few "good places." The "other rooms" of Capote's novel *Other Voices, Other Rooms* are especially relevant. Even before we meet Amy and Randolph, we note that Joel Knox likens himself to Little Kay of "The Snow Queen," who lives in a "frozen palace." Suppose he were taken to such a place: who could rescue him? Entering Noon City with Sam Radcliffe, he notes a "freakish old house" with shattered windows and crazy balcony. Both houses prepare the way for the distortions of Skulley's Landing.

In Chapter Two before he looks at Amy and the bluejay, he has a strange dream. He sees a "knifelike shaft, an underground corridor." He falls into it and then wakes to find a bluejay trying to escape through the window of the bedroom. As John W. Aldridge points out, Joel is like the bluejay, trapped by his relations.[1] Later Zoo, the maid, tells him about the witch who lived close by. One day she fell into a grave and, too weak to climb out, stayed there. Little do both of them realize that this will be their fate. As he begins to become part of the haunted Landing, Joel feels that "he'd locked the door and thrown away the key." Gradually he retreats into the "far-away room"of his imagination where Mr. Misery lives. He meets Little Sunshine who lives in the Cloud Hotel, a palace for narcissism, where "the wide veranda caved in; the chimneys sank low in the swampy earth." He returns to the Landing where "it was as though the place were captured under a cone of glass." There he enters Cousin Randolph's room. It is the place of dreams—the "giant cage."

Joel flees with Idabel to the traveling show, and he

finds the possibility of love with Miss Wisteria. But he cannot abandon his longing for self-imprisonment, which has been instilled in him by Randolph. The climax of this outing occurs in a house in which he hides from the seductive midget. We have a tableau: Joel knows now that he "owned a room" at the Landing with Randolph, and his terror is less than that of Miss Wisteria because she must always travel through "dying rooms." He returns passively to his cousin, without Idabel. The last we see of him is when he approaches the window where the beautiful lady waits. The other rooms beckon forever.

Not surprisingly, other rooms play a large part in Capote's stories. The first time we encounter Sylvia in "Master Misery," she is in the cold, marble-like unnatural apartment of Mr. Revercomb. She is told to return again, presumably to lock herself up in the private world. Her problem is that she has no room of her own. She is trapped with Estelle and Henry: "if she could afford somewhere a small room of her own," she thinks. Sylvia, on her next trip to Mr. Revercomb, looks at a store window in which a "life-sized" Santa Claus is imprisoned. Then she meets Oreilly, who proceeds to tell her that Master Misery "comes down chimneys late at night." No house is safe from invasion by narcissism or authoritarianism. People are always hearing the "step in the attic." Later she tries to remember the peace of her old home, but children's voices disturb her. As Oreilly indicates: "furies inside of us . . . blow open all the doors." Sylvia accepts the other room of her mind at the end of "Master Misery" when, separated from the apartment of Mr. Revercomb, who has *used* her dreams, she cannot face reality.

In "Shut a Final Door" Walter locks himself in a New Orleans hotel room. It has a window but he cannot open it; he is afraid to call the bellboy or leave the room. But the phone voice intrudes. Walter tries to find comfort in the room of the crippled woman: she says, "I mean you said you didn't have any place to sleep." The phone also rings there, and they are disturbed. Likewise in "Miriam" Mrs. H. T. Miller discovers that the "pleasant" apartment is invaded by the ghost-like Miriam. Capote introduces a parallel in the bird-cage incident. After Miriam enters, she uncovers the cage to look at the bird, Tommy, and this makes Mrs. Miller so anxious that she screams out: Don't wake him! When Miriam returns again, intending to stay forever, Mrs. Miller leaves to get help, only to find that she must return to the apartment which, we are told, "was losing shape." Everything looks empty now, "lifeless and petrified as a funeral parlor." The apartment caves in "under a wave of whispers."

Tomb-like imprisonment is evident in "The Headless Hawk." Capote's epigraph is from Job: "In the dark they dig through houses, which they had marked for themselves in the daytime: they know not the light." Vincent, the usual narcissistic hero, walks near a store window that resembles an attic, holding a "lifetime's discardings . . . of no particular worth." The Gothic disarray is a metaphor of his own life. He flees from the strange girl who follows him, returning to his "safe" neighborhood. But he finds that his shadow waits outside for him. The girl not only invades the safety of his apartment but also his place of business. She comes with a painting which has, among other objects, a "miniature gold cage." The cage is where Vincent is going to lock himself. Unable to live without her, he says: "Will you come home with me?" The affair gives him nightmares. He sees in one of them a "hall without exit." The hall contains horrifying figures, men with spider and lizard bodies. He wakes to find the darkness of his own room. Later the room becomes messy: odds and ends cover it. The girl has run away with her demon, Mr. Destronelli, but she has so corrupted Vincent that he cannot sleep, thinking of the "key in the lock." His rooms are now unnatural.

The Gothic interior of the train in "A Tree of Night" is the setting for Kay's descent. Capote emphasizes the decaying "relic," the hot closeness, the stale disarray. The evil parents tell Kay about the mute's act: he is billed as Lazarus, the man buried alive. Their story so impresses her that she remembers her uncle's funeral, thinking especially of his face on the casket pillow. She tries to escape from such visions by falling asleep. However, she dreams of childhood terrors (she is *still* a child), of the wizard who taps at the "window of the house." Kay wakes and then sleeps again, unaware that the woman pulls the raincoat over her head. She is buried alive.

Carson McCullers' rooms are also haunted by self-love, but they are not so bizarre as Capote's. Thus in *The Heart Is a Lonely Hunter* there are no decaying Gothic interiors, merely small-town rooms, drab and unattractive. Mick knows "there was no good place." She has no shelter in which to hum or rest; her family annoys her so much that she has to leave the "outside room" and enter the "inside room." Music and travel and Mr. Singer live there. But the ambivalence between the two rooms is never to leave her. She is not happy in either. Doctor Copeland's room is dark and hushed. His inwardness is resented by Portia who knows that "It don't seem natural why you all the time sitting in the dark." All he can say about his imprisonment is: the "dark suits me." (As I have mentioned, he leaves the room unwillingly to go to his father's house.) Biff's rooms above the New York

Café are also dark and stifling, disturbed by tensions between husband and wife. Actually Biff can only stay upstairs when Alice is in the café. The focal point of the novel is Singer's room. Although we first see him and his beloved, Spiros Antonapoulos, "at home," he has to move to a rooming house after the Greek is institutionalized. To Singer's new room come all those who have no shelter; in a sense, they—like Miriam— transform it into a place of tense disarray. Finally the mute returns there and kills himself.

Reflections in a Golden Eye begins with the controlling image of the army post. The Pendertons, the Langdons, Anacletto, and Private Williams—all the compulsive characters—live in this prison where everything is "designed according to a certain rigid pattern." Each has his own cell in this prison. Private Williams sleeps in a room full of snoring, cursing, or groaning. (He is so withdrawn that he can peacefully eat his candy bar there.) Penderton works late at night in his study, isolated from healthy marriage, locked in abstractionism. Leonora Penderton sleeps without clothes, alone except for the silent Williams, who scrutinizes her. Alison Langdon remains in her bedroom, too ill to travel, except to the asylum: "Where on earth would she go?" The cozy atmosphere created by Anacletto and his Ovaltine party cannot last. The imprisonment of each is so great that when he or she leaves, greater danger is generated. The problem of Penderton is representative: although he works "peacefully" at his desk, he is disturbed by the private who is with his wife, and he finally kills him. In other words, not only *is* each character locked up separately—he cannot find pleasure in his cell because someone invades it. The rigid pattern breaks down.

The Member of the Wedding also uses the image. Frankie, we note, "hangs around" doorways. She wants to enter, but never can. As Oliver Evans notes: "Doorways: that is, always on the threshold of things but never, because of the isolation which is a product of the condition of adolescence, really . . . inside them."[2] The room in which she is virtually imprisoned is the "ugly old kitchen": "the kitchen was a sad and ugly room. . . . And now the kitchen made Frankie sick." Berenice realizes, as Mr. Evans points out, that the kitchen is the world in which everyone is trapped.

Other rooms are present in the novel. Frankie remembers "The House of the Freaks," a long pavilion containing booths in which dwell The Giant, The Fat Lady, The Pin Head—they too cannot leave. Her father is so preoccupied with his watch-fixing that he is trapped in the jewelry store; he always has his head "bent over the tiny watches." The hotel room Frankie visits with her soldier-friend is threatening: in fact, the "silence in the room was like that silence in the kitchen." Going to the room was "like going into a fair booth or fair ride, that once having entered you cannot leave until the exhibition or the ride is finished." She is later trapped in the bus, wishing it could be destroyed. Frankie is, after all, like the "clipped scraps" of cards John Henry places in the stove. The boy himself is buried in the family graveyard in Opelika. Only at the end are the Gothic rooms abandoned: Frankie, now Frances, will enter another house in the new suburb of town.

On the very first page of *The Ballad of the Sad Café* we see the "curious, cracked" house—one side painted, the other unfinished—that seems completely empty, until we notice the face of Miss Amelia at the window. Mrs. McCullers indicates that the boarded-up house (and life) of the woman was once open—and we are into the novelette. In the past Miss Amelia lived alone; like Captain Penderton she often spent the entire night in her shed or study. But after the arrival of Cousin Lymon, the property changed: many people came to the place and the café was born: "For the atmosphere of a proper café implies these qualities: fellowship, the satisfactions of the belly and a certain grace of behavior." These qualities could not last. After Marvin Macy returned to wreak vengeance, he and Cousin Lymon destroyed the café and her life: they wrote dirty words on the tables; they broke the mechanical piano. That is why she now lives in the house. The private world has become a tomb in which the "soul rots with boredom."

Of course, Salinger cannot give us the bizarre rooms of these Southerners. He does present "New York Gothic" in which "ordinary" rooms are suddenly charged with the same kind of meanings. In "A Perfect Day for Bananafish" Salinger describes the hotel in which Seymour and Muriel Glass are staying. We are told that ninety-seven advertising men are there; it is difficult to get a call through. In this environment Muriel sits in 507, fixing her nails. The hotel is so artificial that it cannot shelter Seymour Glass. He must flee from such an alien environment. Later Salinger mentions the rubber float the hero uses as a head-rest. Sybil tells him it needs air—like himself, he thinks. When Seymour discusses the bananafish, he mentions that they die because they're stuck in the banana hole. (Another imprisonment.) After Seymour returns to the hotel he is locked in the elevator with the woman who looks at his bare feet. He proceeds to the room that smells of luggage and nail-lacquer remover and shoots himself. He cannot get out of the prison of self or materialism.

"Uncle Wiggily in Connecticut" also describes the haunted house that materialism and self-love built.

Eloise is not really at home here. Interestingly enough, her Walt was also disturbed by a "room"—the little Japanese stove his colonel wanted him to wrap up exploded in his face. Later Eloise enters Ramona's room, gets her upset, and leaves, "losing her balance." Lionel in "Down at the Dinghy" has been running away from home since the age of two. Mrs. Snell and her self-centeredness have not made home a pleasant place. Lionel finds that he has to find another room: at two-and-a-half he hid under a sink in the basement of the apartment house. Now years later he flees to the dinghy of his father, after he has heard Sandra tell Mrs. Snell that Daddy's a kike. But can he stay there?

The Catcher in the Rye introduces us to "this crumby place," the rest home, where Holden is imprisoned as the result of his problems. He tells us that he could not stand materialistic, phony Pency Prep; they expelled him. Before he leaves, he visits "Old Spencer," his teacher; even in the old man's room, he is "unsafe": He hates the pervasive smell of Vicks nose drops. He blushes when Mr. Spencer reads his answer about mummies on a history test. The mummies reinforce the imprisonment.

Holden finds his room cozy, but even here Ackley comes in to disturb him. Later Stradlater bothers him. He finds some peace in writing the composition about Allie's mitt and remembering his dead brother. One incident is particularly relevant: he remembers sleeping in the garage the horrible night Allie died. Then he broke all the windows with his fist. Holden arrives in New York and rents a hotel room. Again the pattern asserts itself: he finds no peace because he keeps looking at the freakish sights on the other side of the hotel—the hotel is filled with perverts. His room is invaded by self-centered Sunny and Maurice. The trip to the Museum of Natural History is an attempt to find one room where he can be at peace. The museum is associated in his mind with childhood and death. Holden tries to return to it because everything always stayed where it was. But he realizes that he cannot be part of the atmosphere (although Phoebe can), even by putting on his old hunting hat. If only certain things could be put in glass cases and left alone!

Holden returns to his own apartment and enters Phoebe's room (actually D.B.'s) and he "feels swell." He admires the neatness. He explains his departure from Pency Prep using rooms as image: if somebody wanted to come in to join a bull session in somebody else's room, he couldn't; doors were always locked. Holden doesn't understand his ambivalence: he hates open and closed rooms; he hates society and the private world. Although he is happy in Phoebe's room, he has to "beat it." Then he finds other rooms which are unnatural. Mr. Antolini, his former teacher, seems to "make a pass" at him. He flees from his apartment. Much later he returns to his old school to leave a note for Phoebe, and he notices dirty words on the wall. He waits for her at the Museum, only to find the same words. With disgust he says: You can't find a place that's nice.

In "De Daumier-Smith's Blue Period" the narrator finds himself in a crowded bus. He cannot tolerate the passengers or the driver who commands him to move to the rear. De Daumier-Smith prays later for the city to be cleared of people. He wants a solitary room. When he gets his teaching position at the Yoshoto's art school, he is somewhat happy, but he is reminded by looking at the window of the orthopedic appliances shop that he is a transient in a garden of urinals. But the unnatural room—resembling in an odd way Capote's stores—holds a secret for him, a religious message. One evening De Daumier-Smith sees a woman fixing the truss of the dummy; his transcendent experience convinces him that "everyone is a nun." As Gwynn and Blotner comment: "he means partly that everyone, in his aloneness, is like a nun cloistered from the normal contact of humanity." [3]

The other religious stories also use the room. Teddy also has no room of his own: his angry father tells him to get a haircut. Teddy leaves Nicholson after their mystical conversation on deck and goes to the swimming pool to get Booper, his mean sister, as his parents told him. The story ends with Nicholson hearing a scream coming from a small, female child. I assume that Teddy has found peace in the tiled room, after being pushed by Booper.

The tiled room assumes an important function in "Franny," "Raise High the Roof Beam, Carpenters," and "Zooey." (Gwynn and Blotner asked about the significance of the room in these three stories.[4]) In these three stories as well as "Teddy" the tiled room is the ultimate "cloister" for meditation. *No one can intrude.* But this peaceful room is cold, deathlike, unnatural—although Salinger thinks differently. In "Raise High the Roof Beam, Carpenters" the narrator, Buddy Glass, finds himself trapped in a car with Muriel's relatives, who are self-centered and crude. He takes them to his apartment and while they continue condemning his brother, he goes into the bathroom to read Seymour's diary. This room is the cloister. Significantly, Boo Boo, the sister, has written on the mirror a line from a Sapphic epithalamium: "Raise high the roof beam, carpenters. Like Ares comes the bridegroom, taller far than a tall man." Seymour is the bridegroom who demands a new room to contain his "tall" spirituality. The two brothers are thus linked by the image.

Franny is also involved with the tiled room. In her story she is sick of her ego, Lane's self-centered remarks—the whole noisy existence represented by the restaurant. She retires to the rest room to pray. Salinger describes the tile: again it is associated with *satori*, that blessed state of illumination. In the "prose home movie" of "Zooey" we find Zooey seated in a bath reading Buddy's letter about Seymour (sent on the third anniversary of the suicide). He is in a complete state of relaxation, alone with the meaning of life. Some of the spirit of no-knowledge is communicated in the letter (as in the diary or Franny's religious book), and Zooey becomes a changed man. He can even tolerate his mother's later entrance. After Zooey enters Seymour's old room (which still has a listed telephone), he is able to communicate some of his knowledge to Franny, who falls into a deep sleep. There is an unnatural "good place" in the mystical stories.

Turning to Flannery O'Connor's fiction, we find the prisons of the spirit. Rarely are there "temples of the Holy Ghost." In *Wise Blood* there are many prisons. When we first see Hazel Motes, he is on a train. Miss O'Connor describes his narcissistic entrapment in the following way: "he looked as if he were held by a rope caught in the middle of his back and attached to the train ceiling." He has no space in which to breathe. He runs into Mrs. Hitchcock. He is locked up for the night: "He was closed up in the thing except for a tiny space over the curtain." This imprisonment is related to his fearful love of death; the roomette is linked to coffins. Hazel remembers his grandfather's coffin, how he thought at the time it would not shut on his face; he remembers trying to open his young brother's coffin; he remembers that his father "flattened out like anybody else." There are still other rooms mentioned in the first chapter. Two days before getting on this tomb-

like train he visited his old house, which was "nothing
. . . but the skeleton of [a] house." There a board fell
on him and cut his face. It is significant that Hazel
claims the chifforobe; he puts his name on it. This
means that he wants the box as much as he fears it.
At the end of the chapter all the images fuse to pro-
duce overwhelming claustrophobia: "I'm sick!" Hazel
screams. "I can't be closed up in this thing."

The pattern continues. We next see him in the
men's room, where he reads the notice about Mrs.
Leora Watts, the prostitute. He goes there but finds no
shelter because of his imprisonment in The-Church-
Without-Christ idea. Walking the streets he sees other
prisons. A salesman demonstrates a potato-peeling machine: "He stuck a brown potato in one side of the
open machine. The machine was a square tin box
with a red handle." Since this salesman sells his machine near the blind preacher, Miss O'Connor forces
us to associate the narcissistic soul and the potato—
both are enclosed and "mechanized."

What explains Hazel's claustrophobia? He now
thinks of one crucial incident. In his childhood he
went to a carnival where he saw "something white
. . . lying, squirming a little, in a box lined with red
cloth. For a second he thought it was a skinned animal and then he saw it was a woman." The woman
trapped in the box is a symbol of sex. Because he has
viewed her, his mother asks him to repent. He rebels.
The ambivalence—wanting to join the woman, afraid
to—is never to leave his mind. Sex and Jesus are associated; he is trapped by both. Enoch Emery is also disturbed by rooms. He is mystified by the mummy in the
glass case who was "about three feet long. He was
naked and a dried yellow color and his eyes were drawn
almost shut as if a giant block of steel were falling
down on top of him." Note that he—like Hazel—is

buried under things. Enoch, by giving the mummy to Hazel, explicitly identifies the resemblance. Later Hazel dreams that like the mummy (and the woman in the carnival and his family), he is stared at, while buried: "Various eyes looked through the black oval window at his situation, some with considerable reverence, like the boy from the zoo, and some only to see what they could see." At the end of *Wise Blood* Hazel achieves some redemptive freedom. The landlady feels "as if she were blocked at the entrance of something." Her tenant has moved through the entrance and become the point of light.

In "A Good Man Is Hard to Find" The Tower, a restaurant owned by Red Sammy, is a "long dark room" with counter, tables, and dancing space. One of the little children calls it a "broken-down place." Actually The Tower represents the wreck of the spirit. Red Sammy remembers that he once "could go off and leave [the] screen door unlatched. Not no more." Even a dilapidated place offers no shelter. The wife of Red Sammy wouldn't be surprised if the Misfit didn't invade it. Later in the story the Grandmother remembers an old plantation house she had once seen. The house, in contrast to The Tower, seems to be peaceful. It even has a "secret panel" with all the family silver hidden in it. But Miss O'Connor shows us that this house is never reached—furthermore, the Grandmother's self-centered wish to see it causes the Misfit to discover and murder them. Both houses demonstrate the "meanness" of people.

So does the apartment of the Ashfields in "The River." It is filled with cigarette butts and drinks. The son, Harry, has no home: he knows that the apartment is the cluttered world of his sophisticated parents. Contrasted to it is the empty house of Mrs. Cronnin, the babysitter. The most important thing in it is the "colored picture over the bed of a man wearing a white sheet. He had long hair and a gold circle around his head and he was sawing on a board while some children stood watching him." This is the dwelling of "true" religion. Harry is so impressed that he begins to wonder about Christ. But because he cannot cope with its real meaning, he drowns in the river. Again there is no shelter.

In "The Life You Save May Be Your Own" the house plays a crucial part. The old woman regards her "desolate spot" as a proud possession. It is like her daughter. She can do whatever she wants with it. Mr. Shiftlet knows that he can use her narcissism to advance himself: "I'd give me a fortune to live where I could see me a sun do that every evening." By living on her property, he can acquire more things—a car, Lucynell. Mr. Shiftlet says that he can surely sleep in the car—after all, monks "slept in their coffins." Later they have a metaphorical conversation. The old woman tells him that a "poor disabled friendless drifting man" needs a place. When he counters by saying the body is "like a house," he forces her to make the offer: "my house is always warm in the winter." Mr. Shiftlet agrees to marry Lucynell and take care of the house. The points are clear: no one has a good place; the house, like the body, is tinged with sinful narcissism; it becomes a mere commodity. At the end of the story Mr. Shiftlet is still traveling.

"A Temple of the Holy Ghost" also uses the image. The two silly cousins of the heroine make fun of the fact that their nuns call them "temples of the holy ghost." They cannot appreciate the holiness of their bodies. But the precocious heroine is moved by the metaphor. She would like to be in an arena of martyrdom—the great arena in which lions "charged forward and fell at her feet, converted." When the cousins return from the fair, the playground of materialists, they startle her by telling the story of the religious freak who was out-of-place there. They could not see the significance of his ruined temple-body. They laughed. Miss O'Connor gives us a final irony: the preachers from town force the police to close the fair, causing the freak's message to be lost forever. The heroine, however, knows that her temple must be preserved from disruption or ruin. It must shelter the Holy Ghost.

Contrasting dwellings are in "The Artificial Nigger." The room in which Mr. Head wakes is "full of moonlight." It is "dignified" by illusion. The only dark spot in the room is Nelson's cot—he is a mere shadow who must see the light. Mr. Head decides to teach his grandson that the "city is not a great place," filled as it is with corruption. After they board the train, they walk by mistake into the kitchen—they are "displaced persons." The displacement intensifies: Mr. Head finishes his speech on the city sewer system (the "endless pitchblack tunnels" of sin), and discovers that they are lost. Streets become "hollow tunnels"—Hell itself. In front of a suburban house they see the artificial nigger—a "monument" which stupefies them so much that they promise to stay at home, safe in their now-binding narcissism.

The safety of the "established order" is apparent in "A Circle in the Fire." Mrs. Cope is queen of her dominion; she hopes that it will never be disturbed. Ominous whispers at the beginning tell us that the peace of this "good place" cannot last. When Mrs. Pritchard remarks that a woman had a baby in an iron lung, we note the idea of imprisonment. She then tells Mrs. Cope that she had her "arm around it in the coffin." Related to the tomb is the fear of Mrs. Cope that fire may attack the woods, encircle them. So is the image of the poor Europeans "put in boxcars like cattle." The three boys, led by Powell, enter now: they become the circle to enclose Mrs. Cope's property and life. Miss O'Connor writes: Powell "looked as if he were trying to enclose the whole place in one encircling stare." The boys take over the property. (Remember Miriam.) Mrs. Cope begins to feel more uneasy when she hears that Powell once "locked his little brother in a box and set it on fire." One of the boys stretches as if he were "releasing himself from a trap." She screams: this is my place! But it isn't: Mrs. Cope sees the woods set on fire; she hears the boys' shrieks as "if the prophets were dancing in the fiery furnace."

There is one important use of the room in "Good Country People." Hulga dreams of seducing the Bible salesman in the storage barn—the barn becomes a symbol of her private, lascivious, nihilistic world. After they are sheltered there, he opens his suitcase filled with glass eyes, pornographic cards—a Gothic array like Vincent's store window. The suitcase is *his* private world, only revealed to others at strategic moments. The point of the story is that Hulga is trapped in her barn: she can never really leave her world, shocked as she is by the nihilism of someone else.

The opening paragraph of "The Displaced Person" introduces the private domain of Mrs. Shortley. Resembling the old woman who looks at Mr. Shiftlet, she stands like a mountain, rigid, stone-like. Even the sun seems to be an "intruder." The Displaced Persons come and find shelter—poor, discarded, makeshift—with the Shortleys and Mrs. McIntyre, the owner. How lucky they are to have a place like this! Mrs. Shortley thinks, remembering the locked rooms of the concentration camps in the newsreels. The irony is that this new world is as much of a prison for the Guizacs as the old one.

Tensions now disturb the peaceful shelter. Mrs.

Shortley has visions of entrapment; she was "seeing ten million billion of them pushing their way into new places over here and herself, a giant angel with wings as wide as a house, telling the Negroes that they could find another place." Her husband's trick annoys her now: he pretends to swallow a cigarette. When Mrs. McIntyre becomes fond of Mr. Guizac's abilities, Mrs. Shortley's nightmares increase: she sees Polish words all "piled up in a room"—piled up like the people in Europe, the "devil's experiment station." The priest who visits the Guizacs adds to the disturbance. Finally she forces her family to move before Mrs. McIntyre fires her husband. The Shortleys are forced out of their self-centered world.

But Mrs. McIntyre also begins to feel trapped. Her narcissistic order is threatened. As she says to her lazy Negroes: the world is "swelling up" because so many people are filling it; only "smart, thrifty, energetic" ones will survive. She remembers her first husband buried in the graveyard, her second husband now locked in the asylum, and her last probably in some hotel room. Mrs. McIntyre wants to be secure on her property, but her feelings grow. She remembers the Judge's room "left unchanged since his death." Her burdens are tossed onto Mr. Guizac. First she proclaims that *it is her place*, even including the whole field. She does not want to be run over—like the grass near the Judge's "desecrated monument." She tells the priest Mr. Guizac is not satisfactory—he'll have to leave. He has upset things. After Mr. Shortley returns with the news of his wife's death, he gets back his job. He manages to run over Mr. Guizac with a tractor. (Another image of entrapment.) Mrs. McIntyre's mind snaps: she thinks that she is now in "some foreign country." Completely displaced, she retires to her bedroom, where she is occasionally instructed by the foreign priest.

The Violent Bear It Away is filled with entrapment in dwellings. The body itself is haunted. Algene Baliff has called attention to this use of imagery:

> Tarwater is afraid of the "seeds" his great-uncle has planted in him, which "might strike some day" and subject him to the "calling." . . . He senses Rayber, too, as someone who wants to get inside him, to expose and violate his most private parts. The old man himself was once outraged by Rayber when after living with him for three months he discovered that "all the time he was . . . Taking secret tests on me, his own kin, crawling into my soul through the back door." Rayber himself feels he has never gotten rid of the old man's "seeds," and is aroused by Tarwater to a desire to avenge his early "seduction" by "saving" the boy and shaping him in his own image. And Tarwater, thinking himself purged at last of the insidious invasions of both these men, finds himself literally raped by someone he takes to be the "stranger-friend," his other self, who in turn bears unmistakable resemblances to Rayber. Finally, the boy is driven to submit to what he was most trying to escape, the old man himself. In his last ecstasy Tarwater feels the "seeds opening one at a time in his blood": the impregnation burgeons and he can no longer deny its fact. Thus he is taken over and seduced, in these symbolic ways, by all known kin—by the old man, by Rayber, even by himself.[5]

Invasion of self is reinforced by other images. On the first page Miss O'Connor introduces the tomb-like atmosphere by mentioning the great-uncle's grave "with enough dirt on top to keep the dogs from digging it up." From this "private place" we enter the old man's mind. Versed in the prophets, he teaches the orphan Tarwater at home—school is a "prison." The domain of false prophecy is the backwoods: the great-uncle defends it from such intruders as Rayber, who tries to get the boy back. The city where Rayber lives is another prison; the old man was once trapped there: he fled, not wanting to sit "inside anybody's head"—except Tarwater's. Only the coffin offers peace.

After Tarwater flees from his duty by forgetting to bury his great-uncle, he heads toward the city, which is viewed as "a larger part of the same pile, not yet buried so deep." The city is the grave for sinners. The entrance to this grave is a "gaping concrete hole"—a gas station. He talks on the phone for the first time and hears the kind of "bubbling noise" someone would make under water. Finally he enters Rayber's house—an intruder who wants to destroy the atheist's domain. Rayber, the school teacher, begins to instruct Tarwater. He tells him that the old man filled his head with rot. Despite his good-natured appeals the orphan boy simply looks at his hearing aid: " 'Do you think in the box,' he asked, 'or do you think in your head?' " Rayber is so enraged that his heart pounds "like the works of a gigantic machine in his chest." He decides on other appeals, but Tarwater continues to wrap himself in hostile isolation. The "steely gleam in his eye was like the glint of a metal door sealed against an intruder."

The novel moves rapidly to a climax. Rayber decides to take Tarwater and Bishop to the Cherokee Lodge. The ride up there is "oppressively" silent. Tarwater seems to him a "root jerked suddenly out of the ground." Although the trip "was designed to be a trap," the boy has no real feelings on returning to the country near the Powderhead (symbolic?) domain of the old man. Perhaps, Rayber thinks, Tarwater is aware of the "larger grander trap" which left him "barely an inch in which to keep himself inviolate."

Bishop falls into the trap. Tarwater has a sign—the "sun coming out from under a cloud and falling on the head of a dimwit." He decides to baptize the idiot son of Rayber and drowns him accidentally. While this madness is going on, the schoolteacher sits in his dim room, somewhat at peace. When the two don't return, he is disturbed as if "something in him were tearing itself free." And the "beady night noises closed in again."

What of Tarwater? The last two chapters are devoted to his final entrapment. He feels the glare hitting his eyes. His "guts are in his head": he has succeeded in "smothering" the old man's madness, and he is free forever of responsibility. But the invasion continues: visions stick like burrs in his head; black eyes penetrate his head; he is raped by a homosexual. He discovers that the Negro Buford has buried the great-uncle. All these things conspire to make him feel that he must adopt the calling: he smears dirt off the grave onto his forehead. Tarwater has the vision of ecstasy but it is only final entombment in the compulsive design.

The entrapment in private worlds is readily seen in the fiction of John Hawkes. *Charivari* opens with these words: "They slept in separate rooms. A massive dog patrolled the space between." Henry and Emily are not really suited for each other; both are locked in their separate illness. They meet in a "helter-skelter conglomeration" but then Henry descends into the "fictional paradise of his own room." Other images reinforce this claustrophobic narcissism. Butterflies flap their wings under Henry's shirt; voices of his guests descend on him; the hallway seems like an "underpass" in which he is trapped. Emily can't bear the seed inside her. Later Henry feels that the house itself has become a "secretive, unfamiliar place, hatching many subterfuges and maddening familiarities." The cat eats the bird's wing. Fearing that his private world is threatened by marriage and the unborn child, he enters a new house. Now the rooming house is paradise: he is unknown, free; he even has surrogate-mothers to comfort him. But his father invades this domain and returns him to the wedding.

Haunted rooms abound in *The Cannibal*. I have already mentioned the asylum, a controlling image for the entire novel. Balamir leaves the institution only to find shelter in Stella Snow's rooming house. Even the lunatics outside of the institution do not realize they are beyond the "high walls." Hawkes implies that the rooming house is another dwelling of "demented brothers." Each bare room contains someone who lives in a private world: Herr Stintz plays the tuba late at night; Jutta entertains her lovers; Stella dreams of past glory; the Census-Taker believes in "muddled and lopsided" responsibilities. These people return to the institution. Zizendorf, Jutta, and the Census-Taker dance there. The dance is as horrifying as the "fallen segments of plaster from the ceiling," the "chaotic slumber." It is a ritualistic entrapment.

The rigidity of the first section gives way to the "freedom" of the second, which deals with 1914. Hawkes transports us to the brightly-lit restaurant. At first we note the joyous singing, the love for Stella that everyone has. Quite a different house that she possesses! But even here the characters are locked in their private worlds: the Merchant is "barely afloat in the humid atmosphere"; the "pig's tail lay heavily" on Ernie's stomach; Herr Snow dominates his son. The restaurant is an impure temple. Outside the Englishman tells Stella: "I don't really have a home, and in fact, I don't believe anyone has." Stella says that she does. But does she? Her house is a kind of tomb, an "old trunk covered with cracked sharkskin." She is as trapped here as she will be in the future. Because her mother lies in her bed day after day and her father does almost the same, she has no correct image of her strength. Her life is desolate, except for her excursions to the restaurant or to the park. When Ernie and Stella marry, they find paradise in the hotel, in the "upper world." The happiness is short-lived. Ernie's masochism forces him to buy crucifixes: the "crucifixes began to fill the hotel." Then the horrors of war intrude. The next time we meet Ernie, he is trapped in the train, pursued by "monumental dogs." He enters the city, "*das Grab*." In this grave the dream palaces no longer exist—only "dark pleasure rooms" haunted by dogs.

Part Three takes us back to 1945. The destruction of mere pleasure rooms is quickly seen: Hawkes first describes the "pits of excrement," an "occasional shell-case filling with seepage." Zizendorf wants to rebuild: the "tenant must build the house and keep it from sliding into the pool." His new house is his obsession. Can a new house, a good place, be built when the boy gets lost in "underworld tunnels," when Stella's son and daughter-in-law live in a corner of the moving picture house? Zizendorf believes this, especially after the institution is reopened, "revived already with the public spirit."

The Beetle Leg also uses the "other room." The Lampson "buried just below the water level of the dam" dominates the novel. He is the lost ideal or hero for all of the characters who do not realize their own unheroic entrapment: His wife, alone in her misery, keeps her "back to the world and her face toward the red range." She continually goes to the skillet, the "iron of her life," to see if it burns. Nothing matters except the death of her husband. Luke, the brother of the buried man, regrets not having been present when *he* jumped or fell into the dam. Perhaps he regrets not having jumped himself. Camper arrives, vacation-bound, and shuts himself in the town, trying to remember the Slide when a "whole corner of the world fell in." Cap Leech, the missing father, returns. They are in jail. This is why Hawkes elaborates his description of the building, which "with its door open and another locked, kept all men who spit or talked within its walls comfortable on gray lead painted floor or dry cane, confidential, close, by its very smell and heat of confinement, preserved them amidst the circles of the desert." The wife of Camper senses the imprisonment. She looks out of her window and she finds herself unable to move as she sees a "silent figure pressed close to the other side." He is a "Red Devil" who, like his friends, can only break out of rigid adherence to the past by excessive violence. Later she screams "Take me out of here." And Cap Leech realizes that he too has been deceived by accepting the town and family as "my place." *The Beetle Leg* ends with his soliloquy: "Take me there."

In *The Lime Twig* every character is without "proper" shelter. Hencher is introduced returning to the rooming house he occupied with his mother. It is (and was) a dream palace. The suffocating closeness of his relation to the mother is paralleled in many of the images Hawkes uses. Hencher thinks devotion is "sleeping with a wet dog beneath your pillow." He fears the cherubim's limb flying down through the roof, the "fat brass finger in [his] belly." He remembers the odor of smoke "coming round the edges" of the door during the raid, then the pile in which they were buried. Later he enters the womb of the grounded plane.

Margaret Banks usually leaves her rooms once every two weeks for shopping. She returns to find her husband Michael gone; she sits waiting for him. Meanwhile he and Hencher, by trapping the horse (Rock Castle) in the van, trap themselves in the clutches of Larry and the others. The fog covers them: corners are slippery; rats crawl over them. The images of suffocation and imprisonment reach their climax in this chapter as Hencher is crushed to death by Rock Castle: "between the impacted bright silver flesh of the horse and the padded walls no space exists for a man."

The Banks can never return to their dwelling. The thieves go to the rooms and after they do their work, the rooms contain no jewelry, clothing, letters, furniture. Michael himself longs for open air at the track but he is trapped in a steam room, the "brief islands of space" at the track, finally in the oncoming rush of the horses which trample him. Margaret is trapped under Thick's strap. She is bound, her wrists tied together "to the bedpost of brass." Her dreams offer no escape: she dreams of "sitting inside a great rubber tire and rolling down a steep cobbled hill in the darkness." No space exists anywhere.

James Purdy emphasizes entrapment in a less "obsessive" way. His images are not interlocked. Again they are more "routine," less spectacular. In "Color of Darkness" several images establish the confining narcissism. At one point the son, Baxter, throws a bird made out of brown paper into a plant. It "stuck there . . . as though it were a conscious addition." The bird is as stuck as father and son in the pattern. Later Baxter sleeps with an enormous toy crocodile. The sight of the toy shocks the father because it represents cruel power (devouring narcissism?). Significantly, he must take off his clothes, "breathing in front of the opened window." He must free himself of guilt. Still he remains in his pattern; he is "hidden from [Baxter and Mrs. Zilke] in a halo of expansive pipe smoke," which makes him seem "as far away as if he had gone to the capital again." The crucial symbol is the ring. When Baxter almost swallows it, the incident distresses his father. The ring is the symbol of union with convention, with society, and the possible loss of it means that he would have nothing left. By swallowing it, Baxter proclaims his independence and anger. Because he fails in the attempt, he curses his father and kicks him in the groin. The story ends with the father aware of his failure but powerless to change, still trapped: he "nodded from the floor where he twisted in his pain."

In "Why Can't They Tell You Why?" the boy, Paul has retreated into the private world because of his mother's self-love. He usually crouches in corners; he plays near the "close confines of the staircase" with the photographs of his father. His mother decides to teach him a lesson: she throws them into the furnace. As the father-image is imprisoned in the fire, so is Paul forever trapped, not in the institution held out as a threat, but in his own home. That is why he runs feebly, like a "small bird which has escaped from a pet shop into the confusion of a city street." But there are no streets for him.

Mr. Farebrother in "Sound of Talking" is trapped in his wheelchair, using this entrapment as a means of self-pity and subsequent self-love. He holds an old coin "tight" as he does his wife, who wants to assert her freedom. Mrs. Farebrother likes birds; she too wants to fly away. As she tells her story about the pet shop, the "menagerie of birds," she realizes that the story will disturb him even more—he hates pets. One bird said "George is dead, George is dead." Mrs. Farebrother knows that her husband too is almost dead, "his dead weight seemingly scarcely human." But she cannot stop talking; she is trapped by her own words. Mr. Farebrother gives her money for a bird, but she knows he is upset: "She wanted him to want something so that she could want something, but she knew that he would never want at all again." All she thinks now is: he will swell in that chair, "practicing for death."

These "small" entrapments become larger in *63: Dream Palace*. Here the prisons are described at length. On the very first page Purdy introduces the "mansion" of the greatwoman. This mansion is separated from the living; it houses self-indulgence and self-pity. The greatwoman throws "her head back as though suffering from a feeling of suffocation." Parkhearst Cratty looks "like a small but careless hammer." Both narcissists feel guilty because of what they once did to Fenton Riddleway.

In the story proper the images of imprisonment continue to accumulate. Fenton mentions to Parkhearst that he and his brother share a "not-right-kind of place" on 63rd Street. The house offers no peace; it may even have a ghost. Claire Riddleway, the sick brother, admits the house isn't good for him. Thus the house functions as a "dilapidated" trap of the spirit. Parkhearst even views it as representative of his own "shut-in locked life." He—like the two brothers—is encircled by weakness; "if he were opposed he would disintegrate slowly." Before he visits the brothers, he returns to his own house. Bella, his wife, cannot tolerate him, but she loves her imprisonment. At times, however, she looks out of the window "with the intensity of one who is about to fly out into space." After he leaves for 63rd Street, Bella looks out the window at Parkhearst, who looks "like a bug in a desert, hot and sticking to ground, and possibly not even any more alive." (The bugs continue to be mentioned.)

Parkhearst sees that the house looks "rotten and devoured." It is enclosed by a "fence of sharp iron, cut like spears." The windows are boarded up. Inside Claire lies in bed. The house pictures the wreck and confusion of the spirit. Parkhearst decides to rescue the boys from their dungeon and introduce them to Grainger, the greatwoman. Then we see the "dream palace" which has immense rooms, "almost as dark" as those on 63rd Street. It resembles, for Fenton, the ALL NIGHT THEATER, another house where no one pays any attention to anything. Death has a place in the dream palace: there is a memorial room to Russell, whom Grainger loved. (The death room is expanded in the introduction.) Fenton is given Russell's clothes; by wearing them he is trapped into accepting the narcissistic designs of Parkhearst and Grainger.

All the images of suffocation and entrapment reach a climax when Fenton, intent upon dwelling in the dream palace, knows he is trapped by responsibility to Claire: "There would be trouble, then, a great deal of trouble." Claire refuses the special room in Grainger's mansion. Although Fenton flees for what seems a moment, he finds himself in the circle of Hayden Banks, and decides to return to Claire. He strangles him. Then he buries him in the "immense vacant attic with its suffocating smell of rotting wood, its soft but ticklingly clammy caress of cobwebs, the feeling of small animal eyes upon him and the imperceptible sounds of disintegration and rot."

Dream Palace or 63rd Street, new suburb or ugly kitchen, white plantation house or The Tower—all these are prisons of the psyche. The "great, good place" remains an ideal for new American Gothic.

The voyage in new American Gothic opposes the other room. It represents movement, exploration, not cruel confinement. But the voyage is also horrifying because the movement is usually erratic, circular, violent, or distorted. The way out is as dangerous as the room itself. The polarities of room and voyage shrink to one point of horror.

In *Other Voices, Other Rooms* there are many "unsuccessful" voyages. The pattern is established early: it's a "rough trip" to Noon City; "green logs" shine under the water like "drowned corpses"; "rainstreaks and crushed insects" blur the window of Sam's car. The rainfall makes Joel think of a January rain which caused his mother's death. Dusk enters in the City like "queer wine" as Joel climbs into Jesus Fever's wagon. Then he falls asleep—the arrival at the Landing is unnoticed. His slow descent into the underworld is dream-like.[6]

Chapter Two begins with the violent spinning of Joel in his sleep. Before he falls into the crocodile's mouth, he opens his eyes to see the bluejay and Amy pursuing it. The bird flies wildly, trying to escape, but it only scrambles "dazedly" after she swats it. The confused spinning of Joel continues. He tries to relax by looking at the garden but there is a "fiery surface of sun waves." The garden is a wild assortment of seed thrown together. Zoo tells him about her future voyage to freedom in Washington—he says he wants to see snow. (Both voyages end in failure.) As night approaches, restless shadows intrude. Some mysteries clear up as Joel sees more of the Landing. He sees Zoo's scar: it was as "though a brutal hawk had soared down and clawed away" his eyelids—even discovery is violent movement. He meets Randolph who blows smoke rings: his cousin is all circles. He learns "within a dizzy well of stars" that something mysterious is in the house: who is the lady? The sense of being shut-in is strengthened when he sees the shot chicken hawks fall.

Now Joel tries to run away. When he is with Idabel, he imagines "floating lightly away" in the river. But when he kisses her, with "the sky turning, descending, revolving," he breaks her glasses which "sprinkle" the ground like "green raindrops." His first flight is unsuccessful. His dreams are now "winged avenging fish." He runs away with Idabel to the carnival. Part of the journey is perilous: they encounter the springing snake and she in her masculine way kills it; she swings the sword, not Joel. Also they encounter the Negro lovers; Joel knows from her reactions that Idabel cannot be loved. Later they visit the carnival. John Aldridge writes: "The Carnival itself, with its whirling ferris-wheel lights and bursting rockets, is a nightmare catalyst that destroys Joel's sense of reality and prepares him to accept as real the world of the Landing and Randolph." [7] The violent movement is intensified by Miss Wisteria's words: "the world is a frightening place . . . Once I ran away." She is always in flight. And Joel sums up the various flights, thinking that the whole world moves erratically: "moment to moment, changing, changing, like the cars on the ferris-wheel." Only one thing is constant: the self. But immediately after he thinks this, the rain "toppled like a tidal wave." The chapter ends with the flight of Miss Wisteria through "dying rooms."

In the third part of the novel, the spinning movement ceases. Joel has no real longing for freedom. He thinks that he is "guilty." His "stasis" is represented by the "swinging, billowing out" of the sails of the "boatlike sleigh." But danger is still with him at first: his head vibrates; everything goes down. Then the slow rhythm of the rocking chair near his bed, muffles danger. Although Joel is disturbed by Zoo's tale of her voyage—she is raped—he slowly accepts the "gentle jog" of his new self. Capote indicates that like the mule, the boy is "swinging in mid-air" despite his outward calm. Not able to swing forever, he becomes gentle, slow, unhesitating as he walks toward Cousin Randolph.

"The Headless Hawk" begins with distorted, dream-like movement. "Bloated clouds" blur the sun; street voices are "muffled." Vincent feels engulfed, moving below the sea: buses are odd "green-bellied fish." Only the girl comes into focus and forces him to think of immediate flight to the Cape. Then he admits to himself that he is unsure "whether a step would take him backward or forward, up or down." The movement now parallels his growing anxiety. The girl looks at him with "alarming intensity" as she lights his cigarette. Vincent flips away the cigarette and walks into the onrushing traffic. Brakes crash; popcorn bounces and bursts; sparks crackle; "energetic twins" skip rope; and girls "flee like beads of a broken bracelet." Finally he achieves the safety of his home.

The contrasting movements (blurred and frenetic) give an overwhelming impression of strife-torn Vincent. In the painting by the girl a kitten paws playfully a severed head; a hawk brutally descends. Later Vincent discovers her in the midst of booming bulletfire, falling cardboard ducks, savage dancing. He takes her home with him. She brings nightmares. He begins to dream of frenzied movement: of Vincent riding Vincent, of blazing lightening, of odd dancing, and, most important, of the down-rushing hawk which claws him. The chaos is so great that when a butterfly enters the room she has untidied, its beautiful flight—so different from his movements!—annoys him. As it "waltzes" in the air, Vincent tries to slash its wings, but slashes the painting-reflection of himself. In the final section Vincent realizes the nature of his life. It resembles "scattered popcorn." He is still pursued by the girl. As the rain begins to fall, both of them do not run for shelter as do the other people. Trapped "at sea," they wait to be cleansed and destroyed by the "splintered glass."

Capote's wonderful use of movement is also evident in "Master Misery." The "cubes rattling in a glass," the splintering, shattering flowers, the dry "rustling" of Miss Mozart's uniform—all these immediately establish the cold, unnatural voyage of Sylvia. As she leaves Mr. Revercomb's apartment, she enjoys her nature-walk in the park. This voyage also becomes unnatural: two boys appear suddenly to threaten her. Time passes. However, the unnatural movement continues: even the mechanical Santa Claus rocks "back and forth in a frenzy of electrical mirth" and bothers her. Sylvia, distracted by rattling, violence, frenzy, now meets purposeless movement—Oreilly travels with a bottle. All these add up to the circular movement of the plaster girl: "all that effort and the poor girl going nowhere." "Master Misery" ends with the snowfall. (How often rain or snow threatens Capote's characters!) The flakes, "igloo flowers," somehow manage to distort even more the unreality already present. After the clown-like Oreilly has travelled in the blue, after she no longer can visit Master Misery, Sylvia rides on the "white waves of [the] white sea." The "snowy footsteps" of the boys pursue her as she "drowns."

Ihab Hassan writes about the tree-house of *The Grass Harp:* "The tree-house, of course, is the last refuge of innocents abroad. But though it is unlike Huck's raft in that it offers limited opportunities of experience, it is not so much a vehicle of escape, as Capote would have us believe, as a harbor of lost values. For Dolly teaches Collin that the tree-house is a ship, 'that to sit there was to sail along the cloudy coastline of every dream.' " [8] Mr. Hassan maintains that the voyage of Collin, Dolly, and Catherine (together with Riley Henderson and Judge Cool) away from narcissistic Verena and the community broadens their "horizons of *freedom*." [9] Their voyage has a purpose. But it is ultimately unsuccessful. The community—like the two boys or the girl in the raincoat—pursues these travellers, and destroys their purpose. Dolly has to return to her sister; Riley assumes other responsibilities; and Collin travels north to study law. Collin admits that "my own life has seemed to me more a series of closed circles, rings that do not evolve with the freedom of the spiral." Is life a closed circle or a "raft floating in the sea of leaves?"

The voyage is important in Carson McCullers' fiction. In her first novel, *The Heart Is a Lonely Hunter*, there are many voyages. The novel begins with the two mutes, John Singer and Spiros Antonapoulos, walking "arm in arm down the street to work." Their walk is an ordered pattern, a ritualistic procession, which ends with Singer always putting his head on the Greek's arm and looking into his face. Their ideal closeness is lost; the other voyages in the novel are destructive, frenetic, or distorted. Thus a few pages on we see Spiros walking calmly out of the store and urinating in public, bumping into people, and pushing them with his "elbows and stomach." He is sent away to the asylum. Singer then "walks monotonously around the room" or he walks with agitated gait at night, "silent and alone." In the next chapter Jake Blount is an even more confused voyager, talking to Biff about places he had seen—Texas, Oklahoma, the Carolinas. Even his words spout forth "like a cataract." He is, he proclaims, a "stranger in a strange land." We first meet Mick in this chapter; she too is wandering after midnight. Later she spreads her "arms like wings," trying to fly away. She thinks about inventing flying machines for people so that they can "zip" all over the world. But she then descends from the ladder, her dreams earth-bound.

These various hints are reinforced. Mick tells her kid brother, Bubber, that she has nightmares of swimming through crowds of people and being knocked down. The nightmares are painted. She paints ocean storms, plane crashes, sinking boats, and buildings on fire. Portia tells her to find religion—then she won't have to "traipse all around." Jake visits the "motionless merry-go-round" and gets a job operating that wooden circle. Copeland cannot even wander from his house. Singer travels to the asylum and finds Spiros confusingly changed.

Violence erupts. Mick's party changes into a pursuit of the girls by the boys carrying "long, sharp spears of a Spanish bayonet bush." Willie and Highboy, Copeland's sons, go down to Madame Reba's Palace of Sweet Pleasure, and Willie slashes someone with a razor. Bubber thinks "we all gonna drown"; he does as he accidentally kills a child with a stray bullet. Singer's hands twitch while he is asleep. He dreams of his huge-windmill hands, swaying lanterns, and falling downward. Questions flow through Biff, "like the blood in his veins." Copeland descends in the depths "until at last there was no further chasm below." Harry runs away after he and Mick lie together. The violence culminates in Singer shooting himself after he sees the failure of his trip to the asylum. Part III is appropriately concerned with final voyages. Copeland is forced to enter the country house of his father-in-law. He's "got a long way to go." Jake leaves town, running at a "violent, clumsy pace." Perhaps "the outline of his journey would take form." Mick can no longer travel to the "inside room," only to the Woolworth store. Biff swings between two worlds, between "radiance and darkness. Between bitter irony and faith." He sees the "endless fluid passage of humanity through endless time."

Ihab Hassan in commenting on *The Heart Is a Lonely Hunter* says this:

> The tragic confrontation, in this novel much more than in the later works, retains a certain ambiguity, a kind of elusiveness, which the form is incapable of bringing to account. The failure of form can be clarified, I think, with reference to a statement that Mark Schorer has made in *Society and Self in the Novel:* "The novel must find a form that will hold together in some firm nexus of structure the individual human being and the social being. . . ." [10]

I think the novel does have form. Mrs. McCullers uses the polarities of room and voyage to suggest suspension between imprisonment and violent movement; there is no "firm nexus" because these characters have no resting place, no ordered, flexible pattern. *The Heart Is a Lonely Hunter* has what Robert M. Adams has called "open form" or, better yet, "suspended form." [11] Mr. Hassan is closer to the truth when he remarks that the relations, the images themselves, are whirling but they are somehow imprisoned at the same time: a "crazy," rigid kaleidoscope.

The frenzied voyages are in *Reflections in a Golden Eye*. I have suggested in Chapter Two the opposition of rigidity and wildness in most of the characters. Here I will develop images of wildness. Private Williams moves "with the silence and agility of a wild creature or a thief." His wildness destroys the oak tree. He is told by Leonora that down at the stable Firebird has been kicked by a damn mule or mare. Captain Penderton interrupts the peaceful walk of his nude wife by crouching on the stairway as though ready to spring at her. She threatens that she will push him out in the street. Williams, who has watched the scene, walks now "like a man weighted by a dark dream."

In Part II we meet Firebird, foaming, "straining against the bit." Leonora has a "volatile fracas" with him. (But she can control her journey with him, unlike her husband.) Private Williams' "sudden, inexplicable" attacks in the past are mentioned—all these rolling convulsions ended in some disaster. Alison's attack with the garden shears is similar. So is her attitude toward the quail shot and brained by her husband: she bursts into tears. Anacletto dances furiously. Williams is said to let his horses go free. Part III is largely devoted to the violent ride of Captain Penderton. Firebird speeds ahead, uncontrolled, and makes his rider look like "a broken doll that has been thrown away." Penderton loses consciousness. His mind "swarms" with schemes to make Williams, who controls Firebird, suffer greatly. We see Alison and Anacletto. The servant describes his nightmares: boots full of "squirming slithery newborn mice"; holding the baby like a butterfly. Williams' furious murder of a man five years ago climaxes the wildness in this section. So we are ready for the final wildness. Penderton pursues Williams, feeling dizzy. Before he catches up with him, we see Anacletto trying to trip the others he hates by placing bricks at the end of the sidewalk so that they can tumble like ninepins. Major Langdon thinks of running Anacletto "ragged." At last Penderton in a state of delirium shoots Williams. The wild movement comes inevitably to a halt: the Captain slumps against the wall; the private's "sun-browned hands lay palms upward on the carpet as though in sleep."

In *The Member of the Wedding* Frankie Addams walks around "doing one thing and another" (as well as hanging around in doorways). But the sidewalks are very warm, and she returns to the kitchen—"nothing moving any longer." The introductory page gives us the pattern for the whole novel: expansion and entrapment. Frankie dreams of Alaska—of "snow and frozen sea and ice glaciers." Her brother is stationed there. In the past she used to delight in sending him fudge, candy, letters—part of herself. Now he will be married in Winter Hill. (Note the snow, the winter as change of season.) Frankie says: "I've been ready to leave this town so long. I wish I didn't have to come back here after the wedding." Later she plays with the seashell and glass globe with "snow inside that could be shaken into a snowstorm." She is blinded by the "whirling white flakes." Again snow is a new element—free and graceful in movement. As the moths which come out of the August night, which can fly anywhere but "keep hanging around the windows of the house," Frankie is uncertain.

Mrs. McCullers tells us about the girl's past. Frankie thought of the world turning a thousand miles an hour, of the war "happening so fast." She became dizzy. She wanted things to slow down. She decided to donate blood so that she could travel "all over the world." Then the dizziness settled into a "jazz sadness." Frankie tries to tell Berenice about her new desire to leave the town, but the maid does not understand. (Berenice, by the way, has journeyed through snow.) The girl throws a knife—the swiftness reminds her again of the world "fast and loose and turning." How to order things? Others, like Honey and Berenice, do walk "peacefully" to their destinations.

F. Jasmine (her new name), having decided that she will always travel with her brother and sister-in-law, is no longer dizzy; she walks as if in a dream. "The main street, too, seemed . . . like a street returned to after many years." She is no longer jealous of soldiers or the monkey-man, who "came from all over the country and were soon going all over the world." But the glare's "dizzy brightness" returns: the dream-like walk is towards the kitchen. There F. Jasmine hears the piano scale: a "chain of chords climbed slowly upward like a flight of castle stairs; but just at the end, when the eighth chord should have sounded and the scale made complete, there was a stop." Incomplete, odd movement! It adds to the dizziness. Berenice implies in her story that love also causes dizziness: people always travel in circles, searching for an ideal past love. Everyone is "somehow caught." But time moves relentlessly. The frenzy continues in the hotel room; she thinks the lustful soldier is having a fit; she runs away "like a chased person fleeing from the crazy house."

Part Three opens with a brief account of the wedding—the couple don't listen when she says "take me." The journey to Winter Hill is unfruitful. But Frances still decides to "go into the world." Then she changes her mind. The world now becomes not a whirling thing but a "space like an enormous canyon." And the canyon stays with her, even though we see her ready to travel to a new house, even to "pass through Luxembourg when we go around the world together." It is wrong to assume that Frances accepts change—the change of seasons, the change of identity—without her realization that human beings are *not* seasons. They have all the seasons at once.

The Ballad of the Sad Café ends with two types of movement. First we see the dreary town which compels wandering: "Walk around the millpond, stand kicking at a rotten stump, figure out what you can do with the old wagon wheel by the side of the road near the church." This walk is purposeless, boring, almost static. The other movement is that of the chain gang.

The twelve mortal men, although trapped, can expand in singing—their walk is painful but purposeful. Perhaps they represent the only meaningful voyage in Carson McCullers' fiction. Like Spiros and Singer they are bound in a "somber and joyful" procession. Humanity can choose either type of movement, if it can leave the other room.

I propose to spend less time on the voyages in Salinger's fiction because I have already mentioned many of them. They are as erratic and destructive as those found in Capote's and Mrs. McCullers' fiction. Unlike the Southerners, Salinger does not usually insist on a complete pattern, depending as he does on a great deal of conversation. In *The Catcher in the Rye* we have several voyages. The guiding conception is that Holden is "run-down"—the things that happen to him are frenetic. He lacks the graceful order to leap over fences as does the "guy" in the Pencey ads. He loses the fencing equipment on one expedition before the novel opens. He runs, breathing heavily and almost falling, to Old Spencer. The erratic, unsuccessful voyages continue.

In the second chapter Holden first thinks of the ducks. The voyage of the ducks suggests Holden's uncertainty about his own problems: Where can he go? Is he free? Will he be "locked up" in some zoo-like society? Is there any ordered movement? Underlining this uncertainty are two other things. Old Spencer keeps throwing things at the bed and missing it; perhaps the erratic shots annoy Holden because he hates such crazy movement (he indulges in it). And when the boy takes leave of his teacher, he dislikes saying "Good Luck!" He feels that it "sounds terrible," especially to someone who may have an unsuccessful journey.

Holden gets ready for his trip to New York by wearing his hunting hat. He tells Ackley, in a half-serious way, that the hat is worn when he shoots people. The hunting expedition—remember he reads *Out of Africa*—will discover whether people are more than animals. Before he does leave, he and Stradlater talk about Jane Gallagher. Holden remembers that she wouldn't move any of her kings. Why is the incident remembered? Holden is ambivalent: he wants to "hunt" but he also wants to stand still (like the Eskimo); he "expands" and "contracts." Note that the ambivalence is evident when he decides to throw the snowball and not to throw it. Appropriately enough, his departure from Pencey (with his red hat on) is erratic: he almost slips on peanut shells.

In New York Holden continues wondering about the ducks, obtaining little help from Horwitz, the cab driver. He moves from place to place. After his experience with Sunny, he thinks of the past when he used to take Allie as a companion on outings. One day he didn't take his little brother. Holden needs a fellow traveler, someone who can help bear the shocks of moving. The shocks now continue: Maurice hits him, and when he falls, Holden pretends that he is wounded and crawls to the bathroom. He later feels like jumping out of the window. The record he buys for Phoebe falls out of his hand. To soothe himself, he goes home to see her. (Shades of Penelope!)

But even there he cannot flee from the voyage. He remembers James Castle, the boy who jumped through the window. He thinks of the catcher in the rye (earlier he had heard someone singing the lyrics). The images of falling, jumping, crawling, chucking now turn into ideal catching, order imposed on movement. If only Holden could catch himself. The falling continues when he leaves Phoebe. Mr. Antolini tells him that he is riding for a fall. He is afraid that Holden may fall for some unworthy cause. The boy has no time to think about this; he flees from Mr. Antolini. But he keeps falling. Holden *wants* to fall down. The fact that he thinks of dead Allie links falling with the grave, where falling—or any movement—stops. There is one final movement. Holden watches Phoebe on the carrousel. The peaceful movement of the carrousel (so different from the jerky ones in *Other Voices, Other Rooms* and *The Heart Is a Lonely Hunter*) is beautiful, although unattainable for the older Holden. He cries because he is "run-down," not having given shape to his voyage.

The stories contain some effective, isolated images of movement. "The Laughing Man," for example, begins with the "leisurely" expeditions of the Comanches. The Chief guides them. Even though the narrator is lost, he waits confidently for the Chief to find him. Linked to this order, the Laughing Man steals off to the dense forest—there he befriends the animals. The Laughing Man is always on dangerous voyages; miraculously, he survives because of his ingenuity. And as the Chief's relationship with Mary breaks down, the relatively ordered voyages speed up: the narrator trips; Mary Hudson runs away from the Chief. The Laughing Man is trapped; lashed to the tree he can no longer explore. The narrator notes a piece of tissue paper flapping. His teeth chatter uncontrollably because of this *sign*.

"Falling" recurs. In "Uncle Wiggily in Connecticut" Eloise remembers falling in the past when she ran with Walt. She loses her balance, stooping over to tuck in Ramona. Selena's brother in "Just Before the War with the Eskimos" cuts his finger—the cut slowly becomes the symbol of chaos. Lionel in "Down at the Dinghy" is likened to a "shipwrecked" sailor, confused and alone because of Mrs. Snell's friend, Sandra, say-

ing Daddy's a kike. X in "For Esmé—with Love and
Squalor" shakes violently, not able to insert his paper
into the roller properly. The watch Esmé has sent him
had fallen in transit. The grey-haired man in "Pretty
Mouth and Green My Eyes" tries to place the girl's
cigarette in his mouth, but it slips out—he can't
control his movements, having heard her husband lie.
The sun unbalances De Daumier-Smith. The previous
falls become a mystical loss of balance. Teddy falls
into the pool to embrace infinity. Franny's lips move
uncontrollably as she has her vision.

The dangerous voyages of Salinger's characters are
linked to those found in Flannery O'Connor's fiction,
but we must remember that she has the traditional
Christian voyage in her mind. In *The Living Novel*
she writes:

> St. Cyril of Jerusalem, in instructing catechumens,
> wrote: "The dragon sits by the side of the road, watch-
> ing those who pass. Beware lest he devour you. We go to
> the Father of Souls, but it is necessary to pass by the
> dragon." No matter what form the dragon may take, it
> is of this mysterious passage past him, or into his jaws,
> that stories of any depth will always be concerned to
> tell.[12]

That life is a dangerous voyage does not mean it is an
irrational or accidental one; only those who fail to see
the ordered movement are the "fallen" ones.

In the stories we see many destructive images. (I
have already mentioned some.) "A Good Man Is Hard
to Find" begins with the Grandmother not wanting to
go to Florida—the Misfit is headed there: "I wouldn't
take my children in any direction with a criminal like
that aloose in it." The child, June Star, answers: Why
don't you stay at home? Notice that the new voyage to
East Tennessee helps them to meet the Misfit—

ironically, the flight from trouble leads to it. Miss O'Connor deliberately introduces hints to suggest that this voyage is not going to be the usual pleasure outing: she mentions accidents, dumping grounds, "nervous" Bailey, the monkey who bites fleas as if they were a delicacy, the dangerous embankments. After they encounter the Misfit (who is pursued by the police), the same juxtaposition of peace and war occurs: each member of the family walks into the forest and does not return.

"The River" presents Harry's voyage into the forest with Mrs. Cronnin. Before Harry joins the baptism ceremony, he is told by the boys to look at the pigs. When he lifts the board of the pen, "another face, gray, wet and sour, was pushing into his, knocking him down and back as it scraped out under the plank." The pigs roll him over. This hint of violence is intensified by Mrs. Cronnin's mention of Mr. Paradise who (like the Misfit) intrudes to show that he hasn't been healed by baptism. At the place of baptism the preacher declares that the River is "full of pain itself, pain itself, moving toward the Kingdom of Christ. . . . All the rivers come from the one River." The boy is plunged into the water. Because Harry has been imprisoned at home, he decides to return the next day. He drowns himself. The story ends with Mr. Paradise rising like "some ancient water monster" and standing "empty-handed." Again the pleasure outing turns into violence.

When Mr. Shiftlet in "The Life You Save May Be Your Own" says: "the spirit, lady, is like an automobile: always on the move," he is perverting the Christian voyage (as does Harry). The spirit is not *mechanical*. Mr. Shiftlet's statement indicates that he is not to be trusted. All of his movements have prepared us for this. Earlier he allowed the "mystery of flame" to travel dangerously close toward his skin.

Even his face showed violent, "mechanical" movement: it "descended in forehead for more than half its
length and ended suddenly with his features just
balanced over a jutting steel-trap jaw." He called himself a "disabled friendless drifting man." Miss O'Connor suggests that he shifts compulsively, and we are
thus ready for his carefree departure from Lucynell,
ignoring the sign: "Drive carefully. The life you save
may be your own." In the last lines Miss O'Connor
suggests that his voyage will eventually lead to destruction: the "fantastic raindrops, like tin-can tops, crashed
over the rear of Mr. Shiftlet's car."

"A Stroke of Good Fortune," a relatively minor
story, concerns the adventures of self-centered Ruby,
who finds it difficult to climb stairs: the "stairs were
going up and down like a seesaw with her in the middle
of it." Ruby's dizziness, caused by the baby she doesn't
want, represents her chaotic life.

"The Artificial Nigger" contains many erratic voyages. I have mentioned the ironic parallel drawn between Mr. Head and the other spiritual guides, Vergil
and Dante. Mr. Head and Nelson rush to catch the
train, walk into the wrong cars, start walking down the
wrong streets. The boy dashes down the street like a
"wild maddened pony." He falls into the old woman's
way. After Mr. Head denies him, the old man feels: he
was "wandering into a black strange place where nothing was like it had ever been before." His mouth
twitches. After they finally get off the train, they see it
disappear "like a frightened serpent into the woods."
They too have confronted the serpent in the city and,
ironically enough, they think they can forget it in the
safety of their home-prison.

"The Enduring Chill" opens with the voyage home.
Asbury, thinking death is near, returns to his mother
and sister. But this voyage presents as many problems

as his past flight from there to New York. The prodigal son is misunderstood. His vision of "peace" at home is prefigured by the "collapsing country junction"—his "last connection with a larger world [was] vanishing forever." Asbury thinks of the priest Ignatious Vogle who had the spiritual calm that he lacks. Vogle (the bird) and the Holy Ghost fly gracefully, not erratically as he does.

Once home, he obsessively turns to his confused trip to New York: " 'I came here to escape the slave's atmosphere of home,' he had written, 'to find freedom, to liberate my imagination, to take it like a hawk from its cage.' " The bird had been "incapable of flight." When he now looks at the ceiling, he notes a "fierce bird with spread wings," ready for flight. The bird threatens to leap onto him; it seems to represent his chaotic life. Asbury feels dizzy in his dreams; processions lead to the grave.

But these confused voyages are purifying. Asbury Fox finds that although he is not going to the grave, he has cleansed himself. Somehow he has discovered his limitations. And the story ends with a Christian vision of life:

> It was then that he felt the beginning of a chill, a chill so peculiar, so light, that it was like a warm ripple across a deeper sea of cold. His breath came short. The fierce bird which through the years of his childhood and the days of his illness had been poised over his head, waiting mysteriously, appeared all at once to be in motion. . . . [T]he Holy Ghost, emblazoned in ice instead of fire, continued, implacable, to descend.

So we have a reminder of St. Cyril's comment: Asbury has faced the dragon and found the road to salvation. Penance has won. And we can remember Hazel Motes, who travels erratically at first, then moves beyond the door to become the point of light, and Tarwater who moves "steadily" on to the dark city, with his jagged shadow "clearing a rough path toward his goal." All three are Christian soldiers, moving purposefully to their final home.

John Hawkes' characters lack this purposeful voyage. Even in *Charivari*, his first work, we find chaotic movement. Henry Van dreams of drowning, running, a horrible jumping baby. Emily in speaking violently twists her wrist. Their mad party accelerates the movement: no one seems to stop: Mrs. Rice's tongue lashes "about inside her red cheeks" to dislodge some food; Henry's fingers tremble "deliciously"; "internal abdominal rollings, machinations and exertions" are at work; there is "rapid tic-tapping" of feet; canaries fight in a gilded cage; and Noel "canters." Henry's reaction to the party is: "I feel as if there were a hundred persuasions, attachments, curried and combed asses, all tangling themselves about my neck." He flees. Then the storm comes, and Henry feels lost: the rain, "running slime," unbalances him. In the ocean he sees the twisted body of a woman. Later Emily encounters bobbing heads as she runs in the hospital; light shoots in "frenzied beams"; she sees riveters at work. All these movements end when Emily "dances" across the lawn to Henry with the knowledge that some order will be established: no baby is coming.

Albert J. Guerard mentions the "energy, tension and brilliance of phrasing often expended on the relatively unimportant" in *The Cannibal*.[13] The energy and tension *are* crucial to Hawkes' view of life as a "pulsating box"—his claustrophobic characters have been imprisoned so long that when they attempt to move, they move erratically. On the first page Balamir and his insane brothers wander. He sees the pushed bricks, the smashed walls; his brothers "wag" their arms as they chase livestock. As they pursue the livestock, so does the Duke hunt the child. (His hunt is purposeful, direct, but crazy.) Jutta pursues sex: she is in the turn of the road "where nakedness seemed to hang like a hundred apples, pink, wet, and running with the sweet stiff worms." Later the rigid dancing is presented: here movement is automatic, a "clockwork of custom."

In Part Two similar images of pursuit, violent movement occur. Stella's ancestors are said to have run berserk; history runs "thickly" through her. The Merchant slips and falls. Ernie runs after Stella's carriage: he "ran to spend energy"; veins "explode" in his face. Later we see the crazy dogs pursue his train. Herr Snow lasciviously pursues Gerta. Part Three follows the pattern. The Duke gets closer to the boy. Leevey flees from the prostitute on his motorcycle. He runs over the German wasteland like the dogs mentioned earlier. Stella strangles the writhing chicken. At the end Leevey crashes into the obstacle Zizendorf and his disciples have put up. The Duke captures his prey.

There are two underlying voyages in *The Beetle Leg*. The first is the violent motorcycle expedition of the Red Devils. These "wild ones," feeling imprisoned (as do all of Hawkes' characters), expend their troubles through speed—purposeless, nervous, really compulsive. And the inhabitants of the Western town hunt them: the "cowboy's western bark" is heard at the end as warfare erupts between hunter and hunted. Even then violence continues: death almost twitches: "The Devils limped under the red ball rain, suddenly pirouetted into the air or, taking one cleft step, dropped punctured and deflated, arms curling then flat on the ground." The other movement in the novel is also destructive but slow. We are told that the "hill eased down the rotting shale a beetle's leg each several anniversaries." The beetle leg symbolizes the slow, inevitable movement towards ruin, decay, complete stasis. Life then is presented as either Red Devil or beetle leg. The "same discouraging pulse" is without purpose.

And the futile voyage is evident in *Malcolm*. Purdy's characters, so locked in their dream palaces, rarely venture forth, but in this picaresque novel Malcolm is a perpetual wanderer. Remember that he only moves after Mr. Cox urges him to leave the bench of gold. Then he does move like a puppet, first to Estel Blanc, then to Kermit and Laureen, and to the other narcissists. Purdy doesn't show violent movement because all of Malcolm's adventures are sleepy, dream-like—existence is nonvital. As the boy admits: "I'm too sleepy to be scared." It is fitting that he dies in bed, completely worn-out.

Imprisonment in *The Nephew*, Purdy's last novel, is again the dominant image. Alma Mason, the retired schoolteacher, and her brother Boyd—as well as the other characters—are locked in their small-town existence. The only voyager is Cliff, the Mason's nephew, who goes to Korea, admitting as we conveniently discover, that he hates the town and doesn't want to return. From one point of view he is successful: he never does return (presumably he dies in combat). But the voyage is thus simply from "living grave" to the grave itself.

The voyage is destructive in new American Gothic. Capote views it as largely automatic; Carson McCullers stresses spiritual aimlessness; Salinger emphasizes falling; Flannery O'Connor finds hope only in the descent of the Dove; Hawkes sees frenzied pursuit; and Purdy cannot even grant his characters freedom to wander. Thus the voyage is as horrifying as staying at home.

The writers of new American Gothic *view reality itself as deceptive*—hostility masquerades as peace; self-love masquerades as love; children masquerade as adults (or vice versa). New American Gothic uses the reflection—the mirror in which reality is double, cracked, or wavy; only one image is constant—the beloved self. Again the imagery reinforces psychological accuracy.

John W. Aldridge hints at the principle of reflection in *Other Voices, Other Rooms:*

> The characters in *Other Voices, Other Rooms* repeatedly function as metaphors of one another. Idabel, Zoo, and Miss Wisteria are metaphors of Joel; Jesus Fever and Little Sunshine of Randolph and Miss Amy; Jesus Fever and Idabel's father of Mr. Sansom; and, of course, in each case the relationship is reciprocal, so that the metaphor and the person metaphorized are mutually enhanced. The various other devices such as the bluejay, the hawks, the snake, the hanged mule, and Cloud Hotel are also metaphors. The first four are *like* Joel; they demonstrate his predicament.[14]

How appropriate in a novel dealing with adolescent self-love that other people and things mirror Joel, creating a world of reflections—the boy cannot flee from himself; he always sees his likeness! Mr. Aldridge does not note the other uses of the principle.

In the first chapter Capote insists on obscure, distorted reflections. He writes that "luminous green logs . . . shine under the dark marsh water like drowned corpses." The odd light in which logs change shape, in which lilies are as big as a man's head, is the perfect introduction to mystifying reality. Other images are similar: Joel is said to have lived in the past "wearing a pair of spectacles with green, cracked lenses." He also remembers Little Kay, whose "outlook was twisted when a splinter from the Sprite's evil

mirror infected his eye." In Noon City Joel first encounters Idabel, "twisting her face into evil shapes."
He senses unconsciously that she is more of a boy than
he is—reality is upside-down. Jesus Fever is described
as having "yellow feeble eyes dotted with milky
specks." He too cannot see properly. In this distorted
(and distorting world) we encounter doubles: Idabel is
the twin of Florabel (as Joel is the twin of Idabel, Zoo
et al.). The chapter ends with the "smoky" light of the
lamp held by Amy.

The reflections continue: the Landing garden contains five white fluted columns which look like a set of
fingers; it is "glazed." Joel sees himself in the mirror,
which is "like the comedy mirrors in carnival houses;
he [sways] shapelessly in its distorted depth." The
imagery shifts to eyes: he thinks of "picture-eyes that
were not eyes at all but peepholes" in the old house.
He imagines his father peering at him and thinking
that Joel is an "imposter." (The imposter is one citizen
in a world of reflections.) As the kitchen darkens, the
boy sees the walls swell to a "quivering shape." He
walks in the garden, thinking it's all a "crazy trick."
Then he sees the lady in the window: her features
bring to mind his own "vaporish reflection in the
wavy chamber mirror." (Not only is she a double of
Randolph—she is also Joel's double. Mirror within
mirror!) Joel's imagination thrives in this environment. Ferns now resemble "sea-floor" plants; a cabin
looks like a "sunken galleon hulk." Someone keeps
appearing in various costumes and disguises—this
imposter is his father. The sky is a "milkglass." Skulley's Landing, itself, is under a "cone of glass."

Part Two continues the pattern. Joel's haircut makes
him resemble "those idiots with huge world-globe
heads." Amy and Randolph seem "fused like Siamese
twins: they [seem] a kind of freak animal, half-man

half-woman." (The freak is another citizen in the world of reflections.) Mr. Sansom is finally viewed by his son: the father is, as expected, a pair of glazed eyes. Even when Joel leaves the house with Idabel, the reflections are still present. She gives him her glasses which make reality pretty, not freakish; unfortunately, they are broken when the boy and girl wrestle. Idabel's loss of her glasses signifies her introduction to the horribly transfigured world. In the crucial reference to glass, Randolph mentions Narcissus viewing himself in a world of mirrors. All of the images have been building to this revelation: *reality is a distorted mirror for narcissists—they cannot see it as it is. They love distorted images; they force others to reflect themselves.*

After the revelation, the images are not so frequent. Joel sees the "glass bell" of the Landing, the dead blue jay which looks real, the pursuing eyes of his father. He and Idabel confront the snake with "seed-like eyes"; he is powerless before the eyes, having in a sense submitted to the many false visions of the Landing. The incident makes him think: "it was as if their positions of the afternoon had somehow reversed." His former inverted view of Idabel comes to the foreground. Later at the carnival the "real" freaks occupy the stage: the two-headed baby, the Duck Boy, and the stunted Miss Wisteria. Joel is now ready for his surrender to Randolph: he waits for his true reflection, his cousin—the beautiful lady in the "rippling [mirror] of cold, seasonal color."

There are many reflections in "Shut a Final Door." Walter's environment is full of mirrors as distorted as his life. His friend, Irving, is his "little brother," allowing himself to be hurt by everyone; Jimmy Bergman is "two-faced"; his girl friends are duplicates of one another. Walter is never sure of reality, having masquerated for so long. His friend, Anna, also is uncertain; as she says: "Look around this very room: why, you can't burn incense in that fireplace, and those mirrors, they give space, they tell a lie. Nothing, Walter, is ever what it seems to be. Christmas trees are cellophane, and snow is only snow chips." The distortions continue: Walter sees himself in the mirror, where "his face reflected as pale almost as the barber's bib," and knows that he does not know what he wants. Later he thinks of his father's big pair of binoculars. He dreams of the funeral-like cars, the welcome that becomes destructive. His mind propels itself to the breaking point: "it was as if his brain were made of glass . . . he could feel the shattered pieces rattling in his head, distorting focus, falsifying shape; the cripple, for instance, seemed not one person, but several." The cripple, as a matter of fact, is another double: alone, unloved, ill. But she is strong enough to mother him after the terrifying phone rings. The story ends with Walter seeing his feet shining in the transom-light; "the gleaming toenails [are] ten small mirrors, all reflecting greenly."

"The Headless Hawk" has as a partial epigraph: "They are of those that rebel against the light; they know not the ways thereof, nor abide in the paths thereof." Vincent is one of those who don't see the light; his view of reality is fragmented. We first meet him as he walks down the street, thinking that faces are "wave-riding masks." He is searching for the face of his double, his crazy reflection, the girl in the green raincoat; she represents his chaotic, guilt-ridden nature. The girl appropriately wears a man's white shirt; her hair is cut like a boy's. In Vincent's world sex is ambiguous. As she walks past him, he notices her green reflection in a window—that reflection "hardens" and he knows that she will never leave him.

In section two the girl visits him at work, mentioning Mr. Destronelli and bringing her painting. Mr. Destronelli is, as we later learn, her double, the one who inflicts pain—he pursues her as she pursues Vincent; in both cases pursuit is self-willed. The painting conveys something deep: Vincent sees them in it. The headless figure is incomplete nature, destroyed life; the headless hawk is the destroyer (like Mr. Destronelli and the girl). Everyone is cracked: hawk and headless figure. Capote now tells us about Vincent's past. The hero talks to the painting, telling it about his wasted life, how he was compelled to find the girl. He meets her again in a wavy-glass fun-house and takes her home.

At home Vincent "admires his nakedness before a mirrored door." The apartment itself wavers, filled with "delirious" light. The girl mentions that her Granny lived at Glass Hill. All this glass reinforces the shapeless, narcissistic atmosphere in which Vincent makes love to his "girlish" reflection, while she thinks only of Mr. Destronelli. Finally Vincent asks her name—she answers D. J., anyone, male or female. They are happy, imprisoned in greenness. Other images of doubleness now come to the foreground. D. J. remembers the two girls dancing—so free and so close. But Vincent dreams of old horrifying Vincent climbing on young, handsome Vincent. In his dream other people carry "malevolent semblances of themselves." For instance, a "lizard-like" man rides a Negro. A girl imitates Vincent's voice. The hawk from the painting reappears, swooping down. Vincent wakes and thinks: why must he find the "broken image" of himself in those he loves? Later he sees another broken image of himself: a little boy plays in a corner, saying "Whatcha doin', Mister?" as he hides there. Man and boy are one, terrified and alone. Returning to the room, he understands D. J.'s last words: Mr. Destronelli can be anything: a hawk, a child, a butterfly. He feels small (as small as the boy in the corner), remembering a telescope view of the moon. "The Headless Hawk" by elaborating the narcissistic views of Vincent ends with a "universal" note: the sky itself is a "thunder-cracked mirror."

"Master Misery," dealing as it does with ambiguous reality, contains the same kind of reflections. In the first paragraph we see along with the unreal, glass-like flowers, the "snowy" face of Miss Mozart, the nurse of Mr. Revercomb. Snowy signifies all meanings, no meanings. Sylvia is said to be unsure of Miss Mozart: is she really a nurse? Later when she returns to the apartment of Mr. Revercomb, she notes further ambiguity: outside, it is an ordinary house; inside, it is a haven for mad dreamers. In this distorted world Sylvia meets a double in Oreilly. He has also been a patient-victim of Master Misery; he lacks a home as she does; and he is powerless. They meet often in a place with blue mirrors. After his departure (unlike D. J. and Miriam, he flees, not intrudes—a good double?), Sylvia is utterly alone. The whiteness of Miss Mozart is intensified throughout the story by falling snow. Finally the snow fills "every footfall, falling now and here." The ambiguous element, containing all and reflecting none, functions therefore as does the whiteness of the albatross, Moby Dick, the South Pole in A. *Gordon Pym*, and the snow in "Silent Snow, Secret Snow." It contains the secret meanings of the self.

I want to list other uses of reflection. Miriam is, of course, the double of Mrs. H. T. Miller. She has silver-white hair; she has the same name as the woman; she wears a white silk dress and Mrs. Miller's cameo, which contains a trick—reflection. Mrs. Miller buys white roses. She sees a man who shadows her, smiling ambiguously. Snow covers her. In "A Tree of Night" the ice covers the station like some "crystal monster's vicious teeth"—the perfect image to introduce the cruel narcissism we then meet. Not only is it cold— the ice is as "freakish" as the couple Kay sees: the woman is short but she has an enormous head; the man is inscrutable as he later strokes her soft cheek. Doubles are readily apparent: Kay is meeting cruel extensions of herself; her guilt projects itself. The mute and her dead uncle are similar. She steps out of the train, noting that the scenery is familiar, even though she had never made the trip before. The mute is likened to the wizard man of the past. The story ends with the mute's face, reality itself, receding like "a moon-shaped rock sliding downward under a surface of water."

Reflections appear in Carson McCullers' fiction. In *The Heart Is a Lonely Hunter* each character, as I have already mentioned, is a double—Biff, Mick, Blount, and Copeland are broken images of one another. Each is concerned with himself, unconsciously refusing to notice another person. As John B. Vickery writes: there is "a sense of terror aroused by the tragic fact that those who are seeking salvation through companions with whom they might create a community are in fact incapable of recognizing their fellows." [15]

This central situation is reinforced by various images of fragmentation. On the first page we note that Singer and Antonapoulos, although linked arm in arm, are incomplete images of each other. The Greek has half-closed eyelids, a stupid smile. Singer, on the other hand, has "quick, intelligent" eyes. The two are in love, but the love implies cruel fragmentation. Their situation reflects the other relationships in the novel; it "mirrors as well as creates the larger scene in which the characters operate." [16] This is immediately evident in the Biff-Alice relationship. Alice likes lying in bed; she enjoys religion; she knows how a business should be run. Biff is completely opposite. Again the relationship is fragmented, but this very fact reflects the mutes' relationship.

Distortion is evident in physical description. There are many things about Blount "that seemed contrary. His head was very large and well-shaped, but his neck was soft and slender as a boy's. The mustache looked false, as if it had been stuck on for a costume party and would fall if he talked too fast." Biff looks at Mick and sees a "gangling, towheaded youngster, a girl of about twelve. . . . She [is] dressed in khaki shorts, a blue shirt, and tennis shoes—so that at first glance she [is] like a very young boy." Later Biff thinks that in every person there is "some special physical part kept always guarded"—the body itself is fragmented. Biff thinks that for Singer it is the hands; for Mick, her tender breasts; for Alice, her hair; and for himself, his genitals. Jake at one point looks in the mirror and sees "the same caricature of himself he had noticed so many times before." Already deformed, he seems even more so. Copeland's body fights his mind: his tuberculosis destroys his strong true purpose. The distortion is effectively presented in terms of sex by Biff: often old men acquire high voices and "mincing" walk; old women get "rough and deep voices" and grow dark mustaches. He himself wishes he could be a mother; after Alice dies, he uses her lemon rinse. The human being is a freak.

At one point in *Reflections in a Golden Eye* Anacletto paints a bird, "a peacock of a sort of ghastly green. With one immense golden eye. And in it these reflections of something tiny and— . . . grotesque."

The peacock is the deity of the distorted world; it reflects but presumably does not understand the broken images scattered around it. The peacock hovers near Anacletto's mind as does the golden bird which covers Penderton in drug-induced sleep. Not only is the peacock similar to the bird—it is similar to the people who inhabit the world. The people, like the bird, contain within themselves grotesque patterns which they reflect yet do not understand. As John B. Vickery writes: "Williams is the symbolic counterpart of the bird whose golden eye reflects but does not see, save with the terror and despair inherent in its mirror images." [17] Williams resembles all the other characters in the novel in his compulsive-wild reactions. All are "square pegs . . . scraping about the round hole." Sometimes one character tries desperately to become even more like another than is possible—Penderton rides Firebird, trying to become the private.

Thus we have reflections. But these are cut across by inversions and fragmentations. Penderton tries to be Williams, but he is completely unlike the private. (Also he tries to make Williams like him.) Anacletto, Alison, and Lieutenant Weincheck seek peace in beauty, unlike Penderton and Major Langdon who delight in vulgarity. Captain Penderton and Mrs. Langdon "react in opposite ways to the various forms of violence they encounter." [18] Penderton is male and female; Williams is human and animal; Alison's baby is born with joined fingers. Williams is "natural"; Anacletto isn't. These various images of reflection and inverse reflection, like the room and the voyage, tend to make a world in which polarities rule—with the net result of melodramatic intensity.

The Member of the Wedding contains many reflections. The summer is for Frankie Addams a "silent crazy jungle under glass." She views herself in the kitchen mirror, noticing that her "warped and crooked" reflection is freakish: her hair is cut like a boy's; she wears a B.V.D. undervest. She sees that Berenice has one blue glass eye—which stares out "wild" from her colored face. John Henry is also freakish: he is small for his age, but he has very large knees; he wears gold-rimmed glasses. Frankie thinks of her brother whom she had not seen for a long time—his face had become "masked and changed, like a face seen under water."

This abundance of imagery on the first four or five pages is supplemented. Frankie wants to become the couple, to reflect the wedding. John Henry shapes a little biscuit man, a grotesque double. His gold-rimmed glasses are omniscient: he tells Frankie that she is a freak like The Pin Head, The Midget, The Alligator Boy—all the freaks in the sideshow. He "illuminates Frankie's fear that she may become a 'freak.'" [19] Frankie, remembering the freaks, sees their eyes which said: "we know you." She remembers the "queer" sin she committed with Barney MacKean. Frankie even sees her reflection in Charles, the lost Persian cat.

In Part Two after Frankie becomes F. Jasmine, she walks through the town. She looks for the monkey and the monkey-man, thinking that now like them, she will be able to travel. She enters the Blue Moon Café, where the neon lights distort things. Later she finds the monkey and monkey-man who resemble each other in having an "anxious, questioning expression"—this expression is also her own. She sees a reflection, a "dark double shape," in the alley. "The obliquely caught glimpse of two Negro youths unaccountably calls up the image of her brother and his bride-to-be who to her symbolize her own happiness and self-fulfillment." [20] The confused identities mirror her own confusion. Later at home F. Jasmine and Berenice talk

about love. Berenice admits that she tries to find
"little pieces" of Ludie whenever she comes across
them. Unfortunately they usually turn out to be the
"wrong pieces." (Love is cracked reflection.) F. Jasmine meets the soldier and goes with him to the hotel
room—everything there is "crazy."

In Part Three as Frances appears on the scene, there
are less images of reflection because she is less narcissistically distorted. At the wedding she feels "queer":
Jarvis, her brother, gives her a dollar, calls her "Frankie
the lankie the alaga frankie." The night is "queer"
when she leaves the house. For a second she imagines
seeing the couple. The Law Man finds her in the Blue
Moon Café, where in "the blue light she felt queer as
a person drowning." She sees her "own lost face" in
the policeman's eyes. All this queerness prepares us for
Frances' leap into "maturity." Somehow she sees
reality in a new way; only rarely does the queerness
return as when she imagines John Henry with wax
face and arms, a child-dummy. But Mary Littlejohn,
radar, school—normality—capture her. She loses herself.

In *The Ballad of the Sad Café* we see at first the
"curious, cracked look" of the old house. This fragmented appearance is equated with Miss Amelia's
face—a "face like the terrible dim faces known in
dreams—sexless and white, with two gray crossed eyes
which are turned inward so sharply that they seem to
be exchanging with each other one long and secret
gaze of grief." Mrs. McCullers then explains the reasons for the appearances. We are now in the past.
Cousin Lymon enters; everything about him is contrary, ambiguous: he is a stranger, a hunchback with a
"soft and sassy" face. His tubercular skin is both yellow and lavender. And what he says is queer: he is a
cousin, a double, of Miss Amelia (in the same way

Cousin Randolph is related to Joel). He uses as his proof a photograph of two little children who are "tiny white blurs." He proceeds to cry for some odd reason. He is a "perfect match" for Miss Amelia, and the two of them make "one great, twisted shadow."

To reinforce the ambiguity of the situation Mrs. McCullers introduces the disappearance of Cousin Lymon. The town wonders: Has she killed him? The townspeople all look alike now, pale and dreamy-eyed. They symbolize the group in which the single image is submerged. As it turns out, Lymon is completely different from what he was when he first appeared—he is clean; he wears "queerly shaped" shoes, knee-length breeches. He has an "odd manner." He seems even more of an imposter. After we again see Amelia with Lymon on her back (remember old Vincent and young Vincent!), we have a sermon on love. The lover and the beloved are viewed as inverse reflections: the lover tries to make the beloved his mirror-image; the beloved rebels. The attempt of the lover to make anyone a reflection cracks the relationship.

Mrs. McCullers then introduces the Macy brothers. Marvin, Miss Amelia's former husband, is a "mean" fellow who hates the world; Henry, completely opposite to him, is the "kindest and gentlest man in town." (Idabel and Florabel?) Again reality is upside down. Appropriately enough, the first person to see Marvin Macy on his return from prison is Cousin Lymon: they exchange a "peculiar stare" like "the look of two criminals who recognize each other." The hunchback becomes as interested in Macy as Amelia was in himself; he loves the surly man, and wiggles his ears for him. What we have then is a parallel relationship:

> For each of the three main characters is successively lover and beloved. Each, then, is in turn a slave and a

tyrant, depending on whether he is loving or being loved. The refusal or inability of the characters to synchronize their changes of heart produces the interlocking romantic triangles which constitute the plot, while the grotesque comedy arises out of their each in turn conforming to a role they contemptuously rejected in another.[21]

This doubleness is strengthened by other images. The weather is unnatural: there is great heat; snow falls for the first time that winter. Marvin Macy and Miss Amelia battle; Lymon jumps onto her back, causing her to lose. Mrs. McCullers in the one image of Lymon clawing at Miss Amelia's neck shows us how former love is turned into violent hatred. (Perhaps the image comes from Aristophanes' parable in *The Symposium*.) After the two lovers flee, Miss Amelia's eyes cross even more—she has lost her old vision.

The inverse reflection of the three lovers is the chain gang—although these twelve men are bound (as are Miss Amelia, Lymon, and Marvin Macy), they create something new out of bondage—they sing. Their "paradoxical" music creates "ecstasy and fright." [22] And the ecstasy and fright represent the effect of all reflections used by Carson McCullers.

Salinger also uses reflections in his stories. "Uncle Wiggily in Connecticut" contains many such images. Ramona, Eloise's daughter, has two friends, Jimmy Jimmereeno and Mickey Mickeranno (their names are similar), who help her to survive in an alien environment. Jimmy has green eyes, black hair, and no freckles; he lacks parents but he has a sword. In many ways Jimmy is an ideal for Ramona, who is weak, easily hurt by her parents. The fact that Jimmy is killed, then replaced by Mickey, means that the girl is unsure of her ideal or, for that matter, of reality itself. But the intrusion of Ramona's double makes us think of

Eloise's fiancée, Walt. Jimmy and Walt are parallel as
Gwynn and Blotner point out:

> Jimmy stands in the same relation to Ramona as Walt
> does to Eloise—a symbol of the secret image of love,
> unhampered by awful reality. Ramona characterizes
> Jimmy by green eyes, black hair, and no freckles (he is
> unique); by lacking parents (he can be monopolized);
> by a sword (he is a masculine, military hero). Walt is
> unique in his humor and tenderness, is not connected
> with having or being parents, and is an ironical mili-
> tary hero—in that altogether "he felt he was advancing
> in the Army, but in a different direction from everybody
> else" by being about to *lose* insignia in each promotion;
> furthermore, he was really killed while in the Army, and
> if Eloise should tell her husband Lou about it, "I'd tell
> him he was killed in action." [23]

Because Ramona wears glasses (she sees more but
she is wounded), Eloise is more similar to her daughter
than she thinks: she is also wounded. Mother and
daughter and Walt—all people—are represented by
Uncle Wiggily—the Howard Garis rabbit "always
complaining about his rheumatism." [24] The effect then
of the use of reflections is to show the cracked nature
of reality—reality that can only be glimpsed by fresh,
child-like vision.

Much is made of vision in "The Inverted Forest."
Raymond Ford, the poet, is the author of two books—
one of which contains the lines: "Not wasteland, but a
great inverted forest/ with all foliage underground."
His life is that forest as we discover later. The crucial
symbol in the story is his glasses. After Corinne (his
childhood friend) meets him, she notices that only his
glasses saved him from beauty. He wears them, she
learns, because he read poetry constantly in Mrs.
Rizzie's library. The glasses give him artistic, ideal
perspective, but they don't help him to see horrifying

reality or his own underground foliage. This is perfectly clear at the end of the story. Ford is captured by scheming, self-centered Bunny Croft, who makes believe, among other things, that she isn't already married. The symbol of the glasses comes to the foreground in the exchange of Corinne (the former Mrs. Ford) and Raymond. Ford gives up his former vision of life, his ideal glasses. When he doesn't wear them, he looks like a Hollywood star!

The reflections are less obvious in "The Laughing Man." The Chief wears a mask when he tells the narrator and his friends—the Comanches—tales of The Laughing Man. The Laughing Man is an idealized figure, a great criminal, who although disfigured, attains great success in the world. (Like the Chief he wears a "poppy-petal" *mask*.) Why does The Chief tell these stories? Gwynn and Blotner realize:

> The story takes on depth if one assumes that the Laughing Man is [the Chief's] unconscious wish-fulfilling projection of himself. Just as [he] is ugly, but a self-made success who is vastly admired by the boys, so the Laughing Man is ugly ("Strangers fainted dead away at the sight of the Laughing Man's horrible face"), but a self-made success (he has learned to speak with the animals and has "amassed the largest personal fortune in the world") who is vastly admired (by his "blindly loyal confederates").[25]

The failure of the Chief to cope with Mary and the real world forces him to flee into fantasy—fantasy is the mirror where dreams come true. But the ideal is broken. The Laughing Man is uncovered; he is killed.

Salinger does not stop here. As the Laughing Man is an ideal reflection of the Chief, so the Chief is an ideal reflection of the nine-year-old boy. The boy, when lost, waits patiently for the Chief to find him. When the Chief's counterpart is destroyed, the boy, along

with all his friends, is stunned into silence. His counterpart has also been shattered. How could the Chief
do such a thing? After the boy sees the red tissue paper flapping in the wind, he—like Eloise—has a kind
of epiphany: he sees the mask of the ideal. His teeth
chatter because he is now alone without any reflection;
he cannot face reality without "rose-colored glasses."

In the stories reality is an incomplete mirror. So is
idealism. Salinger assumes therefore that the shattered
mirror is an important symbol—adults and children
somehow have to see the horrifying fragments of reality. In "For Esmé—With Love and Squalor" X finds
inscribed in a copy of Goebbels' book: " 'Dear God,
life is hell.' " This comment captures him, and he
writes under it: "Fathers and teachers, I ponder 'What
is hell?' " (from *The Brothers Karamazov*). The crucial
symbol in the story is the watch that Esmé wears. It
belongs to her father, who gave it to her just before she
and her brother were evacuated. It binds her to him
after his death. It is an ideal glass—with magic power.
Esmé mails the watch to X, hoping that it can give
him a new lease on life, pure vision. But it is broken
when X finally receives it. The ideal has been shattered. X senses, I think, that the broken glass, the
fragmented view of reality, is all that he can hope for.
The watch contains "love and squalor"; but it is this
very mixture that can help a person keep his faculties
intact.

Unfortunately, Salinger does not allow his heroes to
accept the splintered glass of reality. His new characters are those who think they view reality in an ideal
mirror which equates all things. They see more glass.
At the end of "De Daumier-Smith's Blue Period" the
narrator has his Experience. Like the Christian mystics
he *sees* the ideal: he is "blinded" as was Paul. When
his sight returns, he discovers a field of enamel flowers.

The distortion is now a transcendent Illumination which helps him to bless even the unreal, the artificial. "Everybody is a nun." Universal light shines on him.

Likewise with Teddy. For him everything—milk, Booper, himself—mirrors God. It is interesting to realize that milk is crucial in the Sunday incident—the whiteness, not disturbing as it was to Sylvia in "Master Misery," becomes the "body" of spirit. Teddy is a "freak"—unlike the freaks in Capote's and Mrs. McCullers' fiction—only because he tries to live a spiritual life in America.

Seymour Glass is aptly named. Although Gwynn and Blotner suggest that his name signifies that "he sees more than others and he shatters like glass," [26] I think the shattered glass is less significant than the ideal one. Seymour's spirit is never broken. In every story this saint *sees* things in a new way. Thus in "A Perfect Day for Bananafish" Seymour equates the blue and yellow for the color of Sybil's bathing suit. (He tries to please her.) Sybil, his double, *sees* the doomed bananafish. Future mirrors are present in this world of prophecy. In "Raise High the Roof Beam, Carpenters" Seymour sees yellow ecstatically. The pattern of mystical Illumination is present in "Zooey." The brother of Seymour, Zooey, *becomes* Seymour when he uses his brother's telephone to instruct Franny about The Fat Lady. Remember that the Fat Lady-Christ relationship is parallel to the Booper-Milk-God vision. The Fat Lady is visualized—she is on the "other side" of the radio.

When we turn to the religious fiction of Flannery O'Connor, we see that one thing does not equal another—she is more aware than Salinger is of the inversions caused by sin. Her fiction emphasizes contrasts, violent juxtapositions, the world upside-down. Only God lacks distortion. "A Temple of the Holy Ghost" is a striking introduction to her work. In it we find a "religious" freak, extremely aware of distortions. The incident describing him is powerful: "The freak went from one side to the other, talking first to the men and then to the women, but everyone could hear. The stage ran all the way across the front. . . . 'God made me this way and if you laugh He may strike you the same way. This is the way He wanted me to be and I ain't disputing His way.'" The freak is a hermaphrodite: he symbolizes the contrariness of men. The girl senses his message; in fact, she sees herself in the freak—a sinful outcast from sinful society.

"The Artificial Nigger" contains many images of reflection. We first notice the moonlight distorting the room; although it casts a "dignifying light on everything," it really holds Mr. Head spellbound—he thinks the chair awaits an order; his pants have an "almost noble air." The old man cannot see clearly, blinded by his "moral mission." Because Nelson, his grandson, has lived with him for such a long time, he also is spellbound. They reflect each other: "They were grandfather and grandson but they looked enough alike to be brothers and brothers not too far apart in age." Mr. Head plans to show Nelson that Negroes are freaks, that they do not reflect white folks. Aboard the train the two of them see their ghost-like reflections in the glass. And although they do not realize it, they see another reflection in the Negro who walks down the aisle—he is as proud as they are. The fact that he is "tan" confuses their vision. The Negro waiters are also proud. The world bound by narcissistic reflections becomes threatening.

After their departure from the train, Mr. Head and Nelson continue on their way. They receive their weight and fortune from the weighing machine: the old man finds that the ticket is a true reflection ("You are upright and brave and all your friends admire you."); Nelson reads that he has a "great destiny." The irony is brutal at this point. Soon they begin to lose their way. Although "everything looked like exactly what it was" to them, the whole point is that it is not what it is. Reality does not reflect their wishes: the unexpected intrudes. Mr. Head denies his "own image and likeness," Nelson, after the policeman comes. He begins to feel some "black mysterious form reach up as if it would melt his frozen vision in one hot grasp." Nelson does not see where he is going. Dusk gathers ominously.

Then the Illumination comes. They see an "artificial nigger" that seems to be a monument built to some Negro. This epiphany means that their former view of reality was distorted. But Miss O'Connor does not stop here. "Mr. Head looked like an ancient child and Nelson like a miniature old man." The roles are turned upside-down; both of them are as "cracked" as the statue. Furthermore, they understand that *all people are miserable, "chipped." They see themselves in Adam.* Now they are "spellbound" in a Christian way as the moon returns; "gigantic white clouds" illuminate the sky. The Illumination makes us remember the fortune tickets—the tickets were right in an odd way! The effect of the entire story is therefore the suggestion of a Divine Plan which turns all reflections —of time, of personalities, of situations—toward a good end.

Wise Blood is largely concerned with vision. Hazel Motes' last name suggests dust particles—that is, clouded vision. Just as he continually sees Jesus before him, so do the other characters stare at one another's eyes, trying to understand and master them. On the train a passenger strains to look at Hazel's eyes: his "eyes [are] what [holds] her attention longest. Their setting [are] so deep that they [seem], to her, like passages leading somewhere and she [leans] halfway across the space that separated the two seats, trying to see into them." In this "curious" world, there is mistaken identity. Hazel thinks he knows the Negro porter; the other passengers think *he* is a preacher. (Later in the taxi " 'You look like a preacher,' the driver said. 'That hat looks like a preacher's hat.' ") Hazel's past was filled with clouded vision. His grandfather, a preacher, wanted him to mirror his gospel messages. So did the mother. The curious thing is that she wore a pair of "silver-rimmed spectacles" that he took along with him when he left home. He carried them "if his vision should ever become dim." Perhaps the glasses indicate that he inherits her Christian vision, even though he rebels against it.

After Hazel gets off the train, he enters the mysterious world where doubles, ambiguities, distortions abound. First he spends a night with Mrs. Watts, the prostitute, who regards herself as "Momma." She is an inverse reflection of Hazel's self-righteous mother. Then he meets Asa Hawks and his "child." Hawks "[has] on dark glasses and his cheeks [are] streaked with lines that [look] as if they had been painted on and faded." This "blind" man is a preacher; his child hands out leaflets. Miss O'Connor spends so much time describing Asa's competitor, the salesman of potato peelers, that we realize the messages of Christianity and materialism are doubled—the crowd cannot distinguish between them. Another double is Enoch Emory, who shadows Hazel and tells him: "You don't never laugh." The boy, as I have already mentioned, mirrors the hero's compulsion, exaggerates it in a comic way. Unlike him, he does not see Jesus, although he admits that "My daddy looks just like 'Jesus.' " The theme is already clear: How can we see the Light in this distorted life?

The reflections continue. Enoch's brain is "shattered": "his brain [is] divided into two parts. The part in communication with his blood [does] the figuring but it never [says] anything in words. The other part [is] stacked up with all kinds of words and phrases." Actually the boy is "non-human." That is why the apes he loves mirror him. So does the mummy mirror him and Hazel. This is clear when "Hazel Motes' eyes [are] on the shrunken man. He [is] bent forward so that his face [is] reflected on the glass top of the case." Later the incident is remembered by Hazel: he dreams of being in a cell, stared at by others. The parallel is strengthened when we recall that he was once punished by his mother for scrutinizing the woman at the carnival. But Hazel continues to *stare*.

Gradually he begins to see the Light. He realizes that Sabbath Hawks is not a child, although she looks like one. He realizes that Hawks is not blind physically—he is an imposter. (He joins all the other imposters: Randolph, Walter, the Chief, Lymon, later Mr. Cox and his friends.) But he *is* spiritually blind. Miss O'Connor tells us about Hawks: "He had preached for an hour on the blindness of Paul, working himself up until he saw himself struck blind by a Divine flash of lightning and, with courage enough then, he had thrust his hands into the bucket of wet lime and streaked them down his face; but he hadn't been able to let any of it get into his eyes." Hazel sees the Light even more after he kills Solace Layfield (the Prophet, unlike himself, of Jesus) and hears his last words: he *does* blind himself. Then Hazel has "the look of seeing something." At the end of the novel the landlady (like the woman on the train) stares into his eyes: She tries to see where he is going, but all she can see is that Hazel is the "pin point of light." Thus the imagery leads from clouded vision, ambiguity, and distortion to epiphany.

In *The Violent Bear It Away* the world is a complex mirror. On the first page we read that Tarwater and his great-uncle live together—the relationship of Mr. Head and Nelson comes to mind. "Tarwater" suggests a muddy view of reality—the fact that he is soon drunk reinforces this assumption. Miss O'Connor, telling us about the past, mentions the "rage of vision" of the great-uncle. The rage is accompanied by the fire which falls in his brain, cleansing but also obscuring it. Along with the fire are the "wheels of light" and the "strange beasts with giant wings of fire and four heads turned to the four points of the universe." The great-uncle thinks he mirrors Ezekiel and the other prophets. After he dies, his eyes are "dead silver." Tarwater knows that he has to bury him, but he hears the voice of a stranger, his rebellious double: death has changed him; he now questions the meaning of his likeness to his great-uncle. The boy's problem is clear: he has to choose between two reflections.

He tries to "keep his vision located on an even level, to . . . let his eye stop at the surface of that," afraid to look at anything for a long time because it demands to be named. But thoughts keep thrusting into his consciousness. He thinks of the idiot son of his uncle Rayber—the child, he imagines, resembles the great-uncle "except for his eyes which were grey like the old man's but clear, as if the other side of them went down and down into two pools of light." Idiocy and prophecy are reflections. Tarwater's thoughts bother him so much that he starts drinking, his eyes "focussing and unfocussing." He decides to burn the house, with the corpse of his great-uncle in it, and the fire pursues him as he runs away from it: he sees "two bulging silver eyes that grew in immense astonishment in the center of the fire behind him."

Getting a lift from a salesman, he imagines that the car is headed in the wrong direction—back towards the fire. But the fire is the "faint glow" of the city—another set of eyes will pursue him there. The distortions continue. Meeks, the salesman, thinks Tarwater is lying—even the "normal" observer cannot see properly. They arrive in the city in "indistinct darkness." The boy is now confronted by the image of Rayber: he sees his eyes, "shadowed with knowledge, and the knowledge moved like tree reflections in a pond." Under the surface a "snake may glide and disappear." He remembers that the old man wanted him to baptize Bishop, the idiot son—he senses that by doing so he is baptizing *himself* for the calling. Not only is Bishop a reflection of the great-uncle—he is also a reflection of Tarwater. Rayber is viewed as a "decoy" set up by the old man, who assumes a "dark shape" as he watches the boy ring the bell. Then Rayber changes his appearance—he becomes the schoolteacher, instructing him to get "out of the darkness." Tarwater later sees both Rayber and Bishop as "inseparably joined. The schoolteacher's face was red and pained. The child might have been accidentally revealed." Thus the end of Part One. Fire, glass, darkness, doubleness, rage of vision—all will be mentioned again.

Now the point of view shifts to Rayber. His vision is also clouded. We are told that he sits near the bedside of Tarwater, "his eyes shining, like a man who sits before a treasure he is not yet convinced is real." The boy looks like a son. (Yet another likeness.) Rayber is frozen because of this "mirror thrust toward him in a nightmare." The teaching process continues. Atheism tries to supplant religion. But the uncle is not a good teacher because he mirrors the old man—he wants to have the old man's eyes, "violent with their impossible vision of a world transfigured," turned on him. One crucial incident now occurs. In the middle of the night the orphan flees from the house to the store-tabernacle of evangelists. There Rayber, following him, sees a girl of eleven or twelve look "directly into his heart." She preaches the Word; he is so "transfixed" that he has to flee. He begins to feel that he is in an alley that "twisted back on itself"—the roles of Tarwater and himself, pursued and pursuer, are "reversed." He knows that the orphan suddenly sees a "compelling vision," that Tarwater, possessing the old man's vision, is going to BURN [his] EYES CLEAN."

At last Rayber decides to take Bishop and Tarwater on an outing which, he hopes, will convince the orphan that he is not looking at things properly. There is a "lost light" at the Lodge. Rayber continues to think of the "invisible country" of silence around him. He hopes they will see the truth soon. Tarwater also wants a "real sign," a miracle of some sort. In the park (before the Lodge incidents) he sees it—he looks at Bishop's "distorted face" and decides to drown him. The sun stops "to watch its reflection" on the idiot's "white head." After this vision, Tarwater is "blinded." When he opens his eyes, he notices two pigeons moving in "drunken circles"—possible doubles of Bishop and himself? At the Lodge the idiot is a "black spot in the glare of his vision." And he is able, with the passive assistance of Rayber, to get rid of that spot.

In Part Three Tarwater is revealed by the headlights of an oncoming car—dazed by his deed. After he tells the driver what he has done, the man answers "Make sense." The incident is parallel to the Meeks one. Tarwater is dazed even more by the "brilliant" morning—he thinks that the sun should be veiled. Even more than in the past, he sees the ghost, the stranger, but he refuses to listen to him. Then he gets another lift from a stranger, a homosexual who rapes him. This stranger, the double of the ghost, forcefully reminds us of the others—of the great-uncle, of Rayber—who also tried to rape Tarwater's mind. Finally the boy's eyes "no longer looked hollow." He mirrors his great-uncle as the fire of prophecy engulfs him and singes his eyes. But in this novel of distorted vision, who is to say that Tarwater really sees the Light or simply the darkness of his own mind?

I turn now to 63: *Dream Palace* and *Malcolm* by James Purdy. In the short novel we are immediately introduced to ambiguous reflections. The great-woman's eyes gape at Parkhearst as though "they would yield him her real identity and why people called her great." Reality is filled with questions of identity and greatness; it is so filled with questions that it is dream-like. Dream and reality are interchangeable as we can see from the following exchange:

> "Fenton Riddleway is vague as a dream to me," the greatwoman said.
> "That means he is more real to you than anybody," Parkhearst said.

Everything is a *riddle*. Only gradually do we realize that this conversation is dead—the two have had this "eternal" conversation many times. Sex too is ambiguous: the greatwoman's face is "shapeless and sexless." It is appropriate that darkness descends as Parkhearst tells the story of Fenton—his voice coming from some far-off space, like some other voice which had "wavered, then had grown, then had sunk into indistinguishable sounds."

Now we are in the "real" world. But even here ambiguity is present. Parkhearst, wandering in the park, pretends to *listen* to people while he *watches* them. It is dark; oddly enough, one shadow stands out—Fenton Riddleway. The boy is ambiguous: he is beautiful but "unsteady"; his eyes are "innocent and getting to be mad." Parkhearst sees his inverse reflection in him, the "wildness and freedom held against his own shut-in locked life." Afterwards he tells his wife about this, but she regards him as some visionary child. When he says that he will adopt his new reflection, not even show it to the greatwoman, Bella knows that he *will*. The ambiguities continue. Parkhearst wonders about the meaning of Fenton's eyes—do they convey any meaning which is "truthful and honest?" Not able to find the house, he thinks it is a trick. He *does* find it and sees the boy "both black and pale" as he stares out the "frosted glass" of the door. Claire may or may not be feebleminded. Is there a ghost in the house? Are they in the right house? Is Fenton all-knowing or "oafish?" The questions are not answered.

Before the boy visits the greatwoman, Purdy describes his adventures a bit more. Immediately we see that Fenton is as disturbed as Parkhearst. He is hurt and delighted when he hits Claire, the only person he loves. He doubts the existence of a Deity. He is young but old. He visits "integrated" taverns, although this is unusual for him. He visits that palace of devotion, the ALL NIGHT THEATER, which has difficult light and strange faces and hands that touch "you as though to determine whether you are flesh or not." Finally he visits the greatwoman. There is music (which is not listened to) and darkness and ambiguous faces—the mansion is like the theatre. The greatwoman decides that Fenton mirrors Russell, her former boy-husband. This hurts Parkhearst who looks at the two of them— they are now "more real and less real than anybody living he had ever known." He decides that Fenton is

"Russell of some kind in the clothes." And he confirms this a bit later after they leave the house, telling the boy: Russell was also *mysterious*.

The novel ends with many ambiguities, parallels, distortions. First Fenton is unaware that he strangles Claire—only when he is ready to bury him does he think that he had killed him. He returns to the house at night (which all through the novel is deceptive or haunted), using matches to guide his distracted way. The attic he enters has a "soft but clammy caress of cobwebs." Fenton, by thinking that animal eyes are staring at him, associates the attic with the theater. He looks for a chest which he has not yet seen. But these odd things are merely the prelude to other ambiguities.

Fenton glances at pictures of a girl in her wedding dress, a man in hunting costume, Jesus and the thieves. All three pictures are reflections. The girl is the Mother they have deserted or the inversion of the false mother, the greatwoman. The man hunting is Parkhearst or Fenton. Claire or Fenton is Jesus—the thieves are Parkhearst and the greatwoman, who steal the spirits of "weak" boys. These suggestions are veiled, like the gauzy veil in the chest Fenton finds. By burying Claire in the veil, he hands his younger brother back to the Mother from whom they have fled —death and marriage are mixed. And the obscenity Fenton utters to Claire as he kisses his "dead stained lips" is the final distortion of nature Purdy employs.

Malcolm also begins on a note of ambiguity. The young man, Malcolm, seems like a foreigner *or* like someone expecting another person. Mr. Cox cannot interpret his meaning, only wanting him to reflect his astrological purpose. All Malcolm does is remain "mysterious." As he is to Mr. Cox, so are the puzzling people *he* meets. Estel Blanc dims the lights, and Malcolm sees Cora Naldi—he is "not even sure at times she was a woman, for she had a deep voice, and he could never tell whether her hair was white, or merely platinum, or whether she was colored like Estel or white like himself." Kermit is first mistaken for a child—he is simply a midget—"one merely felt one was looking at him with the wrong end of the eye-piece." Kermit says Mr. Cox gives anyone his freedom; his tall wife, Laureen, says the opposite. Laureen, as a matter of fact, resembles "ever so noticeably Cora Naldi but of course the two ladies were not at all alike." Malcolm then learns that Kermit was once as innocent as *he* was (before Mr. Cox arrived). In fact after the midget loses his wife, both "youths" agree that life is "pretty scary."

The reflections continue at the chateau of the Girards. Madame Girard, an exact duplicate of Fenton's greatwoman, greets Malcolm; her "makeup was smeared so unevenly across her face and mouth that she resembled a clown more than a woman." She entertains in a "great glass room," where ten identical young men worship her. She begins to see Malcolm as a beautiful young boy, someone who can reflect her narcissistic wishes. Her husband, Girard Girard (even names are double!) sees him in the same way. Later he tells Malcolm that he wants to be his father.

The boy's "unbelievable" adventures continue. He sees Kermit's *shadow* in the doorway—so much is made of the shadow that we begin to realize that all these "odd-plumaged birds" are shadows, as shadowy or nonexistent as Malcolm's father. Madame Girard shadows her face with a riding veil. A few days after, Malcolm meets Eloisa, the painter: she resembles the other narcissists except in one way—she *paints* likenesses of herself rather than molds people. Madame Girard is so irritated by Eloisa that she orates at length about her suffering, her power-giving imagination. She buys Malcolm's portrait from the artist—hoping in that way to capture his likeness.

From this realm of society the boy descends into Melba's world. He meets his contemporaries who are "dizzy." For his marriage he goes to the tattoo palace to gain maturity—like Fenton and his new clothes, Malcolm gets a new skin—that is, he becomes "different." But he does not gain maturity. In perhaps the most significant incident in the novel, he pursues the shadow of his father, but this shadow does not recognize him. The symbolism is clear: Malcolm seeks desperately to see himself in someone, terrified as he is by others wanting *him* to mirror *them*. He wants to find a reflection before he submits to being a reflection. The "father," by refusing to recognize him, accelerates Malcolm's descent. There is no hope at the end of the novel. Mr. Cox, we are told, finds another young man like Malcolm who goes to "25 addresses" and finally eclipses his master. The cycle continues.

The typical hero of new American Gothic moves from haunted rooms in an automatic, misdirected way. Because he sees freaks, imposters, unreal likenesses of himself, he never does discover reality. His vision remains abnormal. Only a cracked, wavy mirror stands before him. Is there anything behind it?

5 CONCLUSION

IN THE PRECEDING DISCUSSION I have tried to chart the important themes and images of new American Gothic. Of course, I have been biased. The following are obviously missing from my discussion: biographies of the writers; usual remarks about decadence; such subjects as religion or time, except where related to psychology; certain unsuccessful stories—Mrs. McCullers' stories, early Salinger as well as "Pretty Mouth and Green My Eyes" and *Seymour: An Introduction*, and many of Purdy's minor stories. I trust that in spite of these conscious omissions, my discussion accounts for the distinctive qualities of Gothic.

Here I note briefly the characteristic styles—the virtues and vices—of the six writers. The following passage is by Capote:

> The gentle jog of John Brown's trot set ajar the brittle woods; sycamores released their spice-brown leaves in a rain of October: like veins dappled trails veered through storms of showering yellow; perched on dying towers of jack-in-the-pulpit cranberry beetles sang of their approach, and tree toads, no bigger than dewdrops, skipped and shrilled, relaying the news through the light that was dusk all day.

The immediate impression is of beauty and lushness. Nature is minutely observed. Details are fresh—for example, the toads are dewdrops. The diction is not hackneyed. But we wonder: why *all* the adjectives? why pathetic fallacy? why the repetition? why the cuteness? why the loss of *meaning* in *decoration?* The defects mirror the general defects of Capote's fiction: the over-elaboration of incident (the Cloud Hotel scene); the forced, pretty symbol (Kay's guitar); the passivity of the characters, all "gentle." But *Other Voices, Other Rooms* and "The Headless Hawk" triumph over their flaws: they demand to be reread for their insight into decay; their memorable images (the headless hawk, Vincent's dream, the carnival, Joel's descent); and their wonderful dialogue.

The following is by Carson McCullers:

> All day there is the sound of the picks striking into the clay earth, hard sunlight, the smell of sweat. And every day there is music. One dark voice will start a phrase, half-sung, and like a question. And after a moment another voice will join in, soon the whole gang will be singing. The voices are dark in the golden glare, the music intricately blended, both somber and joyful. The music will swell until at last it seems that the sound does not come from the twelve men on the gang, but from the earth itself, or the wide sky.

Mrs. McCullers is "romantic" like Capote, but she does not strain for beauty. She is natural in detail and diction ("gang," "hard," "sweat"), yet at the same time she conveys the transcendental, the philosophical (music of the wide sky). She concentrates on—and makes us feel—*pain.* Some defects are evident: the burden of symbolic weight on the gang; the "staged" quality of the scene; the obvious *idea.* But again the defects don't obscure the virtue of Carson McCullers' best work, *Reflections in a Golden Eye,* and *The Ballad of the Sad Café:* the strange "beauty and justice" possessed by her earth-bound "spirits." [1]

Salinger is not interested in nature but stores—the city. He uses the first person to give immediacy, conversational familiarity, but he also offers strangeness. Details are deliberately juxtaposed ("hefty" girl and "wooden dummy") in a startling, fresh way. There are deficiencies: (1) the setting up of a scene (Teddy's pool); (2) the mannerism (endless spiritual *sorties*); (3) the ambiguous, intellectualized symbolism; (4) the monotone. Salinger is at his best in "The Laughing Man," "Uncle Wiggily in Connecticut," *The Catcher in the Rye*, which capture the sudden intrusion of fantasy in the city-world.

Only Flannery O'Connor could have written this passage:

> He stood there, straining forward, but the scene faded in the gathering darkness. Night descended until there was nothing but a thin streak of red between it and the black line of earth but still he stood there. He felt his hunger no longer as pain but a tide. He felt it rising in himself through time and darkness, rising through the centuries, and he knew that it rose in a line of men whose lives were chosen to sustain it, who would wander in the world, strangers from that violent country where the silence is never broken except to shout the truth. He felt it building from the blood of Abel to his own, rising and engulfing him.

Flannery O'Connor can describe nature well (as in the second sentence), but she is really interested in spiritual nature. She is more forceful, satiric, hard-headed than Carson McCullers—and as conscious a craftsman. (Notice the repetition of participles, the simple, biblical phrasing, the thrusting rhythms.) Her fiction is washed in history. All of these virtues overshadow her often-deliberate, literary symbols (as the peacock in "The Displaced Person"), her vague delight in freakishness. *Wise Blood,* "The Displaced Person," and *The Violent Bear It Away* will continue to be read for their "explosive honesty." [2] Of the four writers so far discussed, Miss O'Connor is the only one who has matured a bit more with each new work. Capote's earlier works are much better, truer, than "Breakfast at Tiffany's"; *Reflections in a Golden Eye* is inevitable, while *Ballad of the Sad Café* is somewhat more contrived: Salinger has fled from his Gothic muse into positive Zen. It is hard to predict what Flannery O'Connor will achieve next.

John Hawkes has written:

> Those were certainly dogs that howled. His face pressed against the glass, Ernst heard the cantering of their feet, the yelps and panting that came between the howls. For unlike the monumental dogs found in the land of the tumbleweed, glorified for their private melancholy and lazy high song, always seen resting on their haunches, resting and baying, these dogs ran with the train, nipped at the tie rods, snapped at the lantern from the caboose, and carrying on a conversation with the running wheels, begged to be let into the common parlor. They would lap a platter of milk or a bone that appeared dry and scraped to the human eye without soiling the well-worn corridors of rug, and under the green light they would not chew the periodicals or claw the conductor's heels.

Hawkes returns us to nature that is not recognizable as such—these dogs are *abstractions* of dark drives. His characters are dwarfed by such cruel nature, by running time, by his own imagination. Everything is visual: minor details are scrutinized. His language delights us (as does the obsessive vision) by its freshness, its baroque fancy ("monumental dogs," "glorified for their private melancholy"), and its gracefulness. The passage is truly *new*. But the limitations that appear fully in other works are hinted at here: (1) the am-

biguous symbol—do we really know what the dogs
are? why a train? (2) the care given to the "unimportant"; (3) the literal meaning often obscured—some
passages in *Charivari* and *The Beetle Leg* are incom-
prehensible; (4) the almost-narcissistic delight in private vision; (5) the inhumanity; (6) the straining for
effect (as in the "green light," "carrying on conversation" with the train.) I have spent so much time on
Hawkes' defects because I believe—with Leslie Fiedler—that his fiction gives us more pleasure than most
new writing: the "pleasure of returning to those places
between waking and sleeping." [3] This pleasure is especially apparent in *The Cannibal* and slightly less so in
The Lime Twig. As Fiedler says: Hawkes gives us
"reason's last desperate attempt to know what unrea-
son is; and in such knowledge there are possibilities
not only for poetry and power but pleasure as well." [4]

James Purdy is the author of the following:

> The Tattoo Palace was both severe and cosy—severe
> because it bore every witness to the painful operations
> enacted within—the electrical tattooing needles, the
> bloody rags, the bottles of disinfectant and smelling
> salts, and the bloodstains on the floor; cosy because Pro-
> fessor Robinolte himself, the tattoo artist, was a pleasant
> blond young man who exhibited four front gold teeth,
> and cared for all his customers like members of his fam-
> ily, sending them annual birthday and Christmas greet-
> ings and often advising them on their domestic and
> professional careers, while somewhat behind him soft
> music poured forth, and the air itself was sprayed with
> moderately expensive *eau de cologne*.

Purdy, like Hawkes, writes about *nonrecognizable* nature and city life. He spends less time on visual description. His prose is artless, highly flexible, fluid—notice
that here we have a "conversational" tone, largely ex-
hibited by "moderately expensive," "like members of

his family." Purdy concentrates on incident or effect—
he uses his simple style to lure us into the horror, so
much so that we are not really aware of the style as
instrument. But there are defects. In this passage we
see the emphasis on decoration (why the *eau de co-
logne?*), on the willfully bizarre, the almost-pleasur-
able, "gentle" cruelty, the abstractionism (is the Pro-
fessor really characterized?). Again the defects are not
apparent in much of *Malcolm* and *63: Dream Palace*,
which manage to blend comedy, strangeness, and natu-
ralness, in a disturbing way.

Thus the defects in the six writers are clear: interior
decoration, unnecessary repetition, artificial staging
of scenes, vague delight in freakishness. But the defects
are not so noticeable in the best works of new American Gothic, and these justify the lengthy discussion.
They image the terrors of the buried life: self-love, the
need to destroy community. Until we learn how to
cope with these terrors, Gothic will continue to mirror
and fascinate us.

NOTES

1—Introduction

1. John W. Aldridge, *After the Lost Generation* (New York: McGraw-Hill, 1951), p. 195.
2. Lionel Trilling, "Reality in America," *The Liberal Imagination* (New York: Doubleday Anchor, 1957), p. 15.
3. Richard Chase, *The American Novel and its Tradition* (New York: Doubleday Anchor, 1957), pp. 1–2.
4. Leslie Fiedler, "The Pleasures of John Hawkes," intro. to *The Lime Twig* (New York: New Directions, 1961), p. ix.
5. Ihab H. Hassan, "Carson McCullers: The Alchemy of Love and Aesthetics of Pain," *Modern Fiction Studies*, v, 312.
6. William Van O'Connor, "The Grotesque in Modern American Fiction," *College English*, xx, 346.
7. Quoted on back of *The Lime Twig*.
8. Aldridge, p. 197.

2—Self-Love

1. Hassan, "Carson McCullers," p. 314.
2. Oliver Evans, "The Theme of Spiritual Isolation in Carson McCullers," *New World Writing I* (New York: New American Library, 1952), p. 298.
3. Frank Baldanza, "Plato in Dixie," *Georgia Review*, xii, 156.
4. *Ibid.*, p. 154.
5. Hassan, pp. 315–16.

6. Cf. Horace Taylor, "*The Heart Is a Lonely Hunter:* A Southern Wasteland," *Studies in American Literature,* ed. Waldo McNeir and Leo B. Levy (Baton Rouge, Louisiana: Louisiana University Press, 1960), pp. 154–60. He discusses selfishness.

7. Flannery O'Connor, "The Fiction Writer and His Country," *The Living Novel, A Symposium,* ed. Granville Hicks (New York: Macmillan, 1957), p. 162.

8. Sister M. Bernetta Quinn, O.S.F., "View from a Rock: The Fiction of Flannery O'Connor and J. F. Powers," *Critique,* II (Fall, 1958), 21.

9. Caroline Gordon, "Flannery O'Connor's *Wise Blood,*" *Critique,* II, 9.

10. Louis D. Rubin, "Flannery O'Connor: A Note on Literary Fashions," *Critique,* II, 17.

11. Leslie Fiedler, intro. to *The Lime Twig,* p. xiii.

12. *Ibid.,* p. xiv.

13. Albert J. Guerard, "Introduction," *The Cannibal* (New York: New Directions, 1949), p. xiv.

14. Leslie Fiedler, p. xi.

15. *Ibid.,* p. xiv.

16. Dame Edith Sitwell, "Introduction," *Color of Darkness* (Philadelphia and New York: Lippincott Keystone, 1961), p. 9.

3—The Family

1. Aldridge, *After the Lost Generation,* p. 201.

2. *Ibid.,* p. 203.

3. *Ibid.,* p. 203.

4. John B. Vickery, "Carson McCullers: A Map of Love," *Wisconsin Studies in Contemporary Literature,* I (Winter, 1960), 22.

5. *Ibid.,* pp. 23–24.

6. Paul Levine, "J. D. Salinger: The Development of the Misfit Hero," *Twentieth Century Literature,* IV, 98.

7. Caroline Gordon, "F. O'Connor's *Wise Blood,*" p. 6.

8. Algene Baliff, "A Southern Allegory," *Commentary*, XXX, 360.

9. *Ibid.*, 361.

4—Three Images

1. Aldridge, *After the Lost Generation*, p. 208.

2. Evans, "Spiritual Isolation in C. McCullers," p. 302.

3. Frederick L. Gwynn and Joseph L. Blotner, *The Fiction of J. D. Salinger* (Pittsburgh: University of Pittsburgh Press, 1958), p. 40.

4. *Ibid.*, p. 49.

5. Baliff, "Southern Allegory," p. 360.

6. Cf. Aldridge, p. 204.

7. *Ibid.*, p. 212.

8. Ihab H. Hassan, "The Daydream and Nightmare of Narcissus," *Wisconsin Studies in Contemporary Literature*, I (Spring–Summer, 1960), 14.

9. *Ibid.*, p. 21.

10. Hassan, "Carson McCullers," pp. 317–18.

11. Mr. Adams' book *Strains of Discord* discusses "open form."

12. Flannery O'Connor, "Fiction Writer and His Country," p. 164.

13. Guerard, intro. to *The Cannibal*, p. x.

14. Aldridge, p. 218.

15. Vickery, "C. McCullers: A Map of Love," p. 18.

16. *Ibid.*, p. 16.

17. *Ibid.*, p. 21.

18. *Ibid.*, p. 19.

19. *Ibid.*, p. 23.

20. *Ibid.*

21. *Ibid.*, pp. 14–15.

22. Oliver Evans' word is "paradoxical," "Spiritual Isolation in C. McCullers," p. 310.

23. Gwynn and Blotner, pp. 22–23.

24. *Ibid.*, p. 22.

25. *Ibid.*, p. 25.

26. *Ibid.*, p. 20.

5—Conclusion

1. Evans, "Spiritual Isolation in C. McCullers," p. 310.
2. Gordon, "F. O'Connor's *Wise Blood*," p. 10.
3. Fiedler, intro. to *The Lime Twig*, p. ix.
4. *Ibid.*, p. xiv.

INDEX